Escaping
Extermination

Agi at a concert sponsored by the United Nations
at Carnegie Hall in 1949.

Escaping Extermination

Hungarian Prodigy to American Musician, Feminist, and Activist

Agi Jambor

edited by Frances Pinter

Purdue University Press   West Lafayette, Indiana

Copyright 2020 by Purdue University.
Printed in the United States of America.
All rights reserved.

Cataloging-in-Publication data is on file at the Library of Congress.

Paperback ISBN: 978-1-55753-984-7
ePub ISBN: 978-1-55753-985-4
ePDF ISBN: 978-1-55753-986-1

Every effort has been made to preserve the tone and style of the original text, including in some instances spelling.

*In memory of all musicians
who sustained hope during the horrors of war.*

~

Contents

Foreword

Mika Provata-Carlone

Agi Jambor was born in Budapest in 1909 in a family that welded together the best of what Stefan Zweig would call "the world of yesterday": the comfort and social power of wealth, and the higher vision of a cosmopolitan culture and of a life in art and of the mind.

The daughter of a pianist mother, Jambor was a musical child prodigy, and she would study with such prominent teachers as Edwin Fischer, Zoltán Kodály, and Alfred Cortot. They would infuse her music with a very particular sensibility, which in turn made her into one of the most distinct interpreters of her generation of Bach, Mozart, and Chopin. She recorded several albums for Capitol Records in New York after the war, and was a sought-after soloist, playing under the baton of Eugene Ormandy and Bruno Walter, as well as teaching at several universities and conservatories of music. Music for her was more than a public performance—"I do not play for success; I play to bring life to the composer" an unconquerable eighty-five-year-old Jambor would declare. Music was above all a way of living and of perceiving the world, of interpreting humanity. As a professor of classical piano at Bryn Mawr College, Jambor would pioneer the field of ethno-musicology, insisting that a younger generation of musicians had to "live in the music, recreate the music of non-Western peoples, even if they have no spoken words, no ideas to help them." Seen this way, music contains at its centre an ecumenical potential for eternity; it would be a way out of an insurmountable silence, a forced muteness imposed by the trauma of history and the dramas of individual lives.

Throughout her years, Jambor would maintain that she was able to salvage her soul because she did, unyieldingly, "what I wanted to do and not what I had to." She lived what is by any measure an extraordinary life, enjoying a creative freedom rare for women of her time. She found true love in her first husband, the Jewish Hungarian physicist, inventor, and factory owner Imre Patai, success everywhere she went, and the recognition and satisfaction of being part of the most vibrant and thrilling artistic and academic circles. Yet she was also overwhelmed by tragedy—losing a child, a country, a husband, a previous, rather dreamlike life. What makes her story exceptional is precisely this ebb and flow of triumph and disaster, of blessedness and horror.

Jambor had already lived in Berlin and Paris before World War II; she would return to Budapest with Patai, from where they would be fortunate to flee in a rather colourful manner, under the auspices of forged papers that identified her as a prostitute and Patai as her pimp. Once, the Nazis mistook her pocket metronome for a bomb. Behind this lighthearted scenography of one more twentieth-century Jewish odyssey lies a dark underworld only half-revealed in Jambor's memoir—the other, missing panel of this diptych remains still in the shadows, in Patai's scrupulously kept diary, spanning twenty-seven volumes, that covers the last fifteen years of his life, and perhaps the most poignant and formative segment of Jambor's own.

Her story of survival and persecution under Nazi Germans and Hungarian collaborators is a *catabasis*, a descent into an inferno from which few survived, either physically or psychologically, in their existential integrity and faith in human dignity. What gives Jambor's memoir a particularly evocative resonance and value is the purity of her voice—the unedited quality of her narrative—which brings a world and its ghosts galvanizingly to life.

Also, her quite unique sense of a silent audience, to whom she owes a debt of truth but also hope.

Written in the United States sometime shortly after Patai's death in 1949, Jambor's memoir is steeped in tragedy without being predicated by a confining sense of introspection—by the sense of entrapment that is the terrible undertone of the Holocaust, of postwar words, and of all attempts at a conceptualisation of the horror, at an analysis of evil, and the retrieval of a state of (im)possible normalcy. It has an arresting clarity as World War II history; as a Hungarian, Central European story; as a chapter of Jewish memory, the tale of a great pianist, of music; as a portrait of America in its age of perhaps brightest greatness and innocence; and especially as an engrossing, empowering female narrative. It is also an unmistakable, moving ode to a husband, to an age of irrecoverable happiness, to a world shaped and informed by everything with which Europe's Jewish heritage could enrich it.

Jambor's text has a particular poignancy as a chronicle not only of disaster, of total devastation, but also as a Jewish *via dolorosa* to a resurrection and revival of a tradition. Jambor writes of a universe of nightmares—of evil and annihilation—she provides an almost cinematographic testimony of how a world of wonder and possibility was lost, perhaps beyond retrieval. To that, significantly, she adds her formidable talent for life and reconstruction, her tenacious conviction that the legacy of humanity, of art, of Central European values, and especially of Hungarian Jewry could and should be given a new lease of existence—a New World and promised land.

In this respect, Jambor does not speak as a single voice; she does not even speak with the dual resonance of her husband's own experience, trauma, and insight. Her voice and her trajectory, her periplus and arrival, reverberate with the echoes of each individual member of a legacy at home and in exile across the world that are still relegated to the realm of nebulous ambiguity. Jambor's story throbs with the pulse and urgency of many others—the Jewish and/or Hungarian voices that were lost or that had to embrace another language and way of existence: from Joseph Pulitzer, who led a previous generation, to the novelists Sandor Márai, Imre Kertész, György (George) Konrády, Margit Kaffka, Péter Nádas, and Magda Szabó, or the eerie cohort of Hungarian Jewish intellectuals who perished during World War II: Lászlo Fenyö, Endre Friss, Ignác Gábor, Oszkár György, László Lakatos, László Nagy, Károly Pap, Márta Sági, and Antal Szerb to name only a fraction. László Moholy-Nagy and Lajos Kasak, André Kertész, Brassaï, and Robert Capa feature among the artists who defined a new modernity, while Béla Bártok, Zoltán Kodály, Georg Solti, Antal Doráti, Annie Fischer, András Schiff, or Zoltán Kocsis would lead in turn the new paths of music—to follow Liszt and, for those with a taste of geography and genealogy, Johann Sebastian Bach. To read Jambor's memoir is to yearn for the company and stories of so many others, with whom she crossed paths or shared a history, a sense of creative purpose, or a vision.

Memory is not simply the reverse of forgetting; it is an antidote to an oblivion that erases consciously or unwittingly, that gradually dematerialises human presence and experience. It is most crucially the opposite of denial: a resistance against the deliberate assault on the value of truth, on the meaning of human suffering (or happiness), on the very ethics of being. Imre Kertész would say that

> the decades have taught me that the only passable route to liberation leads us through memory. But there are various ways of remembering. The artist hopes that, through a precise description, leading him once more along the pathways of death, he will finally break through to the noblest kind of liberation, to a catharsis in which he can perhaps allow his reader to partake as well. But how many such works have come into being during the last century? I can count on ten fingers the number of writers who have produced truly great literature of world importance out of the experience of the Holocaust. We seldom

meet with the likes of a Paul Celan, a Tadeusz Borowski, a Primo Levi, a Jean Améry, a Ruth Klüger, a Claude Lanzmann, or a Miklós Radnóti. More and more often, the Holocaust is stolen from its guardians and made into cheap consumer goods. Or else it is institutionalized, and around it is built a moral-political ritual, complete with a new and often phony language.[1]

Jambor did not seek to write a work of great literature, yet what she has bequeathed to us is certainly great memory, a counter-measure to what Elie Wiesel saw as perhaps the ultimate crime perpetrated by Nazi Germany: "At Auschwitz, not only man died, but also the idea of man. To live in a world where there is noth-ing anymore, where the executioner acts as god, as judge—many wanted no part of it. It was its own heart the world incinerated at Auschwitz."[2]

Agi Jambor's memoir has a rare quality of humanity; an unyielding power as a testimony and as a final tribute, as a ges-ture of mourning and of closure in the aftermath of an unhealable wound. It is especially a gesture of openness and of potentiality, which are only attainable through the conscious, constant act of remembering and reconstruction.

NOTES

1. Imre Kertész, "Who Owns Auschwitz?," translated by John MacKay, *The Yale Journal of Criticism* 14, no. 1 (Spring 2001): 267–72.
2. Elie Wiesel, *Legends of Our Time* (New York: Schocken Books/ Random House, 1968), 18.

1

Peaceful waters turn choppy

It was in 1938 that we moved to Holland.

My husband, Imre Patai, was the first man in Hungary to start manufacturing radio tubes. His enterprise, the VATEA, was started in a little basement, but grew so fast that the Philips Company became interested and bought it. My husband then became an employee of this Dutch company, and they built a large research laboratory for him in Budapest. As far as I know, this was their only large laboratory at that time outside of Holland.

My husband was the inventor of the colloid-coated cathode, which was adopted by Philips in all their radio tubes, and I believe by other companies too. Beside working in the Philips Laboratory, he also had a private laboratory of his own, in which he worked on a variety of projects. I remember, for example, that he worked on kidney stones in collaboration with a physician friend of his. This work stopped in 1938 when this doctor immigrated to America and we moved to Eindhoven, Holland, where my husband organized and headed up the television research of Philips.

In December 1939, after war broke out in Europe, Imre felt compelled to leave Philips. He felt, and rightly, that the Germans would eventually occupy Holland, and then Philips would be turned over to war production in aid of the German war effort. He realized that it would then be too late for him to leave Philips, so he decided to leave too early rather than too late.

1

We moved to Amsterdam at the invitation of Professor Clay, and my husband worked with him on cosmic rays. Professor Clay was a very fine man, and Imre loved his work at the university. The war reached us in Amsterdam five months later, in May 1940. The breath of war had touched us many times before the German invasion. Shortly after the Western powers declared war on Germany, in September 1939, I was playing a concert on the radio in Hilversum. Imre could not come with me on that occasion, so he was listening to it in Eindhoven. In the middle of my playing a Chopin scherzo, a man stepped on the stage and stopped my playing with the announcement: "German planes are overhead." Everyone thought that it was an air raid, but the Germans were only flying over without intending to attack. The people ran out to the street, not to miss seeing bombs falling.

The concert was disrupted and not resumed again. The worst of it was that Imre, listening on the radio, heard only that I suddenly stopped in the middle of the scherzo, and nothing more. He was terribly worried, fearing that something serious had happened to me, until I called him.

Another interesting episode happened a little later. The Dutch Army was mobilized and the Queen asked for volunteer scientists, artists, and other professional people to educate the young soldiers. I thought that it was a splendid thing to carry on constructive education in those bad times, so I immediately wrote offering my services. I stated that I was a foreigner but my sympathies were completely on the side of the Dutch. Within twenty-four hours my letter was answered, and my offer was gratefully accepted. The letter was signed by Princess Juliana. One evening soon after that an army captain appeared with a car and drove me to an unnamed place (the location of the troops was a military secret), where in a canteen I gave a concert to the soldiers. Since they were mostly farm boys, unacquainted with classical music, I had to explain to them in Dutch what I was doing, which wasn't easy for me! They appeared to have enjoyed it, and so did I. That late-night trip was afterward repeated in different camps in the country.

Probably the most touching incident of this period was my visit to the island of German children. The Dutch government had donated an island for young German children between the ages of ten and twenty, who were refugees from concentration camps. Volunteer artists made trips to the island to help educate the children. I volunteered and went to the island to give a concert.

I have always believed in trying to stimulate an active interest in music by participation rather than solely a passive interest by listening. So after I finished playing I asked if they would not like to play, saying, "doubtless some of you have studied music before getting into concentration camps. If you would like to come up and play for each other it would be enjoyable for all of us." One young man around eighteen or twenty—a nice-looking youngster with clear blue eyes and light blond hair—came up. He told us how he had started a career as concert violinist before he was put into a concentration camp because he had some Jewish blood in him. He was tortured there, he was hung up in such a way that his shoulders were dislocated, and they broke all of his fingers. He had not had a violin in his hands since that time. The superintendent of the camp offered him his violin. There was no music available, so he improvised. He played wonderfully. Then a girl came up who had studied piano in her earlier life. She proved to be extremely talented—so talented that I told her to come to me in Amsterdam when she could and I would give her lessons. (She did come every week; some friends paid her fare and I gave her lessons free.) While I was playing that night airplanes approached and air raid warning signals were sounded. I paused and asked the kids whether we should stop the concert and go to the shelter. They replied, "We would rather continue. If we must die, we would rather die with music," and so we continued the concert. I heard later that after the Germans occupied Holland they killed all the youngsters on the island.

At the time of the German invasion we lived in the house of an elderly couple. And here we felt pretty confident that we were safe and felt convinced that these old people were not Nazis. Prior to coming here we had moved several times while in Amsterdam because each time we met circumstances that aroused our suspicions of the people with whom we lived. The only person of whom we were suspicious in this house was the butler. He was a silent man and gave us the uneasy feeling that he was a spy. He acted in the manner of a butler in a play, always moving about silently and watchfully. I always had a creepy feeling whenever he entered the room; my nerves told me that he must surely be a Nazi spy.

The house itself was a beautiful old mansion, and it seemed to afford us the security we were seeking. The night before the Nazis invaded Holland we were having a musical party at the home of some Dutch friends. That day the Queen issued a proclamation to the effect that Hitler had promised to respect her country's neutrality. We were feeling happy over this news that evening and our hope rose that nothing would happen to Holland. But I remember that in the midst of our complacent talk the first cellist of the Amsterdam Symphony Orchestra remarked dryly, "Don't be so happy. You may wake up during this very night and find that Hitler is standing on Rembrandt Square."

That was about 11:30 or 12:00. The party broke up about this time and everyone went home. Around 3 a.m. my husband woke me, saying, "I think the cellist was correct." He had heard a lot of explosions and many airplanes. I said to my husband a silly thing, "It is only some military maneuvers, go back to sleep," which I did. But my husband turned on the radio while I slept and lay listening. Again he awakened me, saying, "Amsterdam is being bombed by the Germans." And so we began to dress, thinking we would have to go down into the cellar—before the thought occurred to us that in Amsterdam there are of course no cellars since the city is built on water. So we did the only thing we could: we stayed right in our room. My husband remarked after a while, "This is an historical moment. I will begin to write a diary," and he sat at the desk and began to write down his observations. He kept his diary until his death nine years later, or more correctly, until the day before he went to the hospital where he died. As the bombs fell, he wrote, and I just stayed in the bathroom trembling. People said the next day that these were the biggest bombs and the largest number of airplanes that we would probably ever see in our lifetime. How wrong they were! That morning Imre said that he must go first to the university because there was very valuable equipment there for measuring cosmic rays, and he must pack it immediately.

Shortly before this, Professor Clay had received money from the Dutch government to go to the Dutch East Indies in connection with his work of measuring cosmic rays. He wanted Imre to go along as his coworker, and it was decided that I would go along as the cook for the expedition. I had been a concert pianist since I was eleven years old, concertizing all over Europe for many years. By this time I had gained recognition as a concert pianist over a good part of the Continent. Even so, I would have been glad to go along with Imre and Professor Clay as their cook. However, things developed fast and the trip never materialized.

While we were packing the cosmic ray equipment a terrible bombing came. We rushed into the basement of the university. It was one of the very few buildings that had a basement. Characteristic of the good-natured Dutch people, a pot of coffee and cookies awaited us. This took the edge off our fear, and we all sat down and enjoyed the refreshments, having a spirited discussion on science and philosophy. Suddenly, Professor Clay arrived and said that all the students who could blow glass must come upstairs and blow syringes for blood transfusions. There were a great many people injured in the bombing who were in need of blood. A sudden silence fell over the group. This was the first time that we realized fully that we were in the war.

We heard then that in the next block from where we were living, a direct hit had been made and many children had been killed. We immediately wondered if our home was damaged too. We tried to go home, but this was not easy because everybody was now under suspicion. People were stopped on the street and asked to say *Scheveningen*, a word no one but a Dutchman could pronounce. They were looking for traitors and, rightly or wrongly, they assumed that the traitors must be foreign. I felt humiliated when the guard stopped me on the street to search my pockets to see if I was carrying a gun.

When we reached home we found there a changed atmosphere. The old couple were now very silent and the butler had become very much alive and active. He became very talkative and asked everybody their feelings toward the Germans. The two German refugees who had been living there were preparing to leave. The butler was now suddenly very friendly, but the old couple shut themselves up in their rooms and did not come out except during air raids. Everybody in the house came into our room during air raids as we were on the first floor.

There were frequent bombings and lots of excitement. One of the nights was particularly exciting. On this night somebody rang the bell at the gate. Everybody, with the exception of my husband and myself, lived on the second and third floors of the house. It was not our custom to open the gate because there was a janitor who did that, but on that night no one came in to answer the ringing, so finally my husband said that he would have to go. Returning he said that it was the Dutch Night Guard, and they told him that German parachutists had come down and two of them landed in the garden of the house in which we lived. Imre and I vengefully grabbed some sticks and went into the garden to beat whatever Germans we found there. We searched the whole garden and were disappointed that we could not find a single Nazi to beat with our sticks. It must have been a funny sight. Imre was a short, thin man and I was still smaller. I guess a Nazi could easily have handled the two of us even without a gun. But we were too excited to think of that. After our fruitless search I rushed upstairs to the old couple's apartment and told them to come down to help search the house for the parachutists. Naturally, they refused to come down. About three hours later there came another air raid and the couple came down to our room, as they had done during previous air raids. We had suffered about eleven air raids during the eight days. This was the first time that the elderly couple brought along some luggage with them. We believed that the parachutes were in their luggage and that the parachutists were hidden by them somewhere in the house. The butler asked them to open their luggage but they refused.

The Battle of the Netherlands lasted only eight days. The day the Germans occupied Amsterdam, our butler and the two German refugees disappeared. The old couple turned out to be ardent Nazis who owned, or were stockholders in, a number of German factories. Shaken by this we left as fast as possible. Before leaving, however, we heard on the radio a great speech by President Roosevelt. It was now forbidden to listen to American and British broadcasts but all the same our friends sneaked into our room at 3 o'clock at night and listened to Roosevelt's speech with us. It moved us tremendously. I was never touched by a speech quite as much as on that occasion.

During the siege I became aware of a quality of the Dutch that endeared them to me, namely, that they were able to retain their sense of humor under the most trying circumstances. One example of this was in connection with the taping of all windows, which was ordered as soon as the German bombings started. Everybody had to tape their windows to prevent shattering of glass and injuries from flying splinters. So the good Dutch people began to exercise their self-expression according to their profession. One hairdresser displayed on his show window a head, beautifully coiffured, made entirely of paper tape. The grocer arranged his tape in the shape of a ham. My husband expressed himself by making geometrical designs on our windows.

For four months of the German occupation we lived in Holland. Imre borrowed a copy of *Mein Kampf* from a friend. He had the idea that great historical events must be subjected to a dispassionate scientific study. He felt that he must do this, forgetting our own fate in order that it may serve later generations in understanding the happenings of those days. This was the reason for keeping his diary. He said, and I well remember it,

"Now that involuntarily I must leave my own profession, I have to use my scientific mind to observe human nature during a world catastrophe." He read and wrote practically all day and night. When he finished Hitler's book, he said, "Why did we not go to America twenty years ago?" And he went again to this friend of ours and borrowed all the works of Nietzsche and tried to get all the books that could have influenced Hitler. Thus he worked out gradually the chain of ideas that he believed were the moving force in Hitler's insane actions. He wrote a hundred pages on Hitler's book alone. This study ended in a paper that I hope I can translate some day; it is a deep psychological analysis of war and its effect on the human soul. From this paper there came another result too. After a long search he found a theory that goes a step further than Freud's study in this field. The psychoanalysts of Hungary later examined, accepted this theory, and put it to actual use. Thus did Imre, unable to continue his physical research, spend his days and nights reading, studying, thinking, and writing at home. Uninfluenced by fear, or his own personal feelings, he tried to serve humanity this way, as he had done before in his science.

2

Living from hand to mouth

While we lived in Holland we were not molested by the Nazis because we were Hungarian citizens. At that time Hungary was a neutral country, or more correctly, a nonbelligerent ally of Germany. After four months we returned to Hungary. We arrived home with all our furniture and books. The Germans took all of our money but allowed us to take our furniture and books back, which we sent home in forty boxes, but when we reached Hungary and went to collect them, there were thirty-nine boxes. A box that contained part of our silver was missing.

This was actually a stroke of good luck for us. The boxes were insured, so we filed a claim for 300 guldens for the missing box, and we collected the money. Since we arrived in Hungary absolutely penniless, this money was a Godsend to us. Much later, after the war, a lady wrote to us from Holland, notifying us that the missing box had been found, but since we had collected anyhow we let it go at that.

Before leaving Holland one was supposed to declare all the gold one possessed. I guess we were the only ones in Holland who obeyed this decree. The Germans threatened dire consequences, including the death sentence, for everyone who failed to declare. Imre said he would rather die than give his gold to the Nazis. But I was terribly frightened and persuaded him to comply. Thus we arrived in Budapest without enough money for carfare.

Before we went to Holland Imre and I owned a beautiful house in Budapest, which we had had to rent long ago, and it was still rented. As a matter of fact, Hanna Honthy, one of the most famous Hungarian actresses, rented it. Because of this, when we returned to Budapest we had no place to live, so we went to a hotel. In our hotel room my husband said, "I can't stay without research work, I must start to do something." It came into his mind that in Holland once when he was ill I had observed a strange behavior of the milk under certain conditions. At the time he didn't believe it, and we forgot the whole story. Now talking to me in our hotel room Imre said, "Why not see if your observation was right? It goes against all the rules of chemistry I can think of, but I should like to try it anyhow." We bought a thermostat and some little bottles, and he began making a laboratory in the good-sized closet we had in the room. The maid in the hotel came to me once and said, "Your husband must be a suspicious person. He always locks his closet." Of course, that wasn't the reason at all. Every scientist locks his laboratory when he leaves it. The results of Imre's experiments proved that my observation was right. He improved on my observations and developed a new kind of buttermilk. Then we went from dairy to dairy in an effort to sell our new milk. Finally, my husband sold it, but the very day he did so came the milk rationing, and we were once again with empty pockets, empty closet, and just a little hotel room. (Incidentally, after we came to the United States, Imre applied for a patent on this buttermilk, and this application is still pending.)

The situation was pretty unsatisfactory, so we decided to convert our house into a laboratory. We asked Miss Honthy to move out, which she very graciously agreed to, and Imre set up his laboratory there. Ever since he started working as a young man, he had always put aside a certain percentage of his earnings to buy various pieces of laboratory equipment. He had the idea that he would retire at sixty and spend the rest of his life doing the kind of research he himself wanted to do in his own laboratory. This equipment had accumulated throughout the years, and the basement of the house was full of it. Now Imre changed the entire house into a laboratory with the exception of a single room, which we reserved for ourselves to live in during the summer. We found an apartment in Budapest where we lived the rest of the year.

Our house must have been a remarkable sight to onlookers. We kept two goats to give us milk, partly for the buttermilk experiments, partly for our own consumption. Then we kept a whole rabbit farm there for certain biochemical experiments of Imre's. We started with two rabbits and read up on the handling of rabbits in all the books we could get ahold of. We followed every rule and direction with the utmost care and diligence, but as the weeks passed we had no more than the original two rabbits. Finally, we got desperate and called a veterinarian to tell us what was wrong with our rabbits. It didn't take him long to diagnose the trouble. He announced with a broad smile that both rabbits were "gentlemen." We quickly remedied the situation and there was no reason to complain after that for a while, at least not until the house became so full of rabbits that we couldn't move around.

Eventually Imre did find a group of people who were willing to finance his plans. They gave him enough money for a laboratory where he was able to work on his inventions and even set up a small plant where he could produce things. At that time, most Hungarians still considered themselves neutral. In the few neutral countries of Europe most people lived in the illusion that their country would remain neutral. No one liked to face the facts because if we did we probably would have committed suicide. Imre decided that he would try to manage his affairs so that the factory would be ready to go into full production when the war ended. Of course, he miscalculated, and the war overtook us. So he began a very slow and a very careful sabotage in his factory, long before the German occupation. The things produced in the factory were themselves harmless and of no military value, such as lightning rods. And, after all, lightning rods cannot win a war. He also produced a new kind of instrument to relieve the overloading of telephone lines.

Since Imre wanted to go slowly with his research, he took time out to study chemistry at the university. In Holland, while doing his research work on kidney stones, he came to the conclusion that he did not know enough chemistry, so he utilized this period of "involuntary laziness" to bolster his knowledge. He also worked in his laboratory, in collaboration with Dr. Tarjan, on a new kind of photocell, a joint idea of the two of them. Dr. Tarjan was a very dear friend of ours and a wonderful chemist. He had worked in Berlin most of his life, but when Hitler came to power he returned to Hungary. Imre made also a tiny quartz lamp that could be swallowed by a patient and used for internal radiation treatment of various diseases.

At this time I had permission to give concerts anywhere I wanted, but I did not act on this permission. Let me try to explain the situation. When Hitler became ruler of Germany, he immediately started the persecution of the Jews. Everybody who had at least one grandparent who belonged to the Jewish race was considered a Jew. After Hungary came under German influence, the Nuremberg Laws were adopted in Hungary too. This was not a popular measure in Hungary. Intermarriage in Hungary between Jews and non-Jews was very frequent, especially in the middle and upper classes. The wife of the regent himself was half-Jewish, thus even the children of Nicolás Horthy fell under the Nuremberg Laws.

Both Imre and I had "non-Aryan," tainted blood in us. However, I fell under an exception clause. I was an "Olympicon," because I won the fifth Prize at the International Chopin Competition in Warsaw in 1937, before the war. Thus I was allowed to concertize freely, but Imre and I decided that I should play only in places where Jewish people had permission to play, and in other places only for charity. There was one small hall where Jews were permitted to play. By this time the Jews were excluded from most of the life of the nation, and a great many of the men were in labor camps. The little concert hall was always filled, mostly with Jews.

(I should like to interject here that I use the word "Jewish" in the same sense as the Nazis used it, namely, in the racial and not the religious sense. Thus, some of the high dignitaries of the Catholic and Protestant churches in Hungary, including a number of bishops, were Jews; i.e., they had at least one grandparent who belonged to the Jewish race.)

At one of the concerts where I played, in the first row sat an American notable, Counsellor of the American Legation Mr. Bonbright, who had recently been posted to Budapest. After that the Bonbrights faithfully attended all of my concerts. We became very good friends; they were among the finest people I have ever known. I will never forget the last lunch I had with the Bonbrights when they had to leave Budapest. Mr. Bonbright said he saw all around him in the city streets people who looked like intellectuals shoveling snow and they all wore yellow armbands. He inquired what it meant. I explained that it meant that these people were almost all Jews or partly Jewish, and they were in a labor camp. He looked at me and his eyes were full of tears. He said, "Promise me one thing, if you too have to wear a yellow star you will be proud of it. And remember that you have a friend in America who is proud that you are not crushed under this." The departure of the Bonbrights was one of the saddest days in my life, for with their leaving Imre and I had a feeling of complete loneliness and despair. When our best friends left, it felt like the doors of a prison closing in upon us.

3

Fate closing in

In the middle of 1942 I was expecting a child, and my husband's idea was that future parents had to be prepared for this job as we prepare ourselves for a profession. He went into the depths of studying this subject as he had gone about studying Hitler's soul and the soul of a Nazi. He wanted to observe what goes on in the soul of a man before he becomes a father. He started with his rabbits, and kept a diary on them, observing their attitudes hour after hour. He delved with ruthless objectivity into his own soul and that of his friends. The result was a psychological study, a new step in deep analysis. I gave it a name, the Laius Complex. Laius was the father of Oedipus. This study was generally accepted and used by psychoanalysts.

Every Monday evening during 1940 through 1942 I conducted a choir. The meetings were held in our apartment. It had two aims. One aim was to help to maintain morale and spirit in those difficult times. I always felt that active participation in music is more elevating than merely passive listening, especially for amateurs. My second aim was to earn a little money, since my husband was earning very little at that time. As I recall everyone paid one pengö an evening—about twenty cents at that time. I had no money with which to buy music, so I had to write out all the scores myself, which was pretty hard work.

15

My other activity was connected with an orphan home. A lady I knew had founded a little home for forty-five children whose parents had been killed, in many cases before their eyes, in Czechoslovakia, Poland, and Germany. They were brought somehow to Budapest without knowing our language or anything of the country. Among them was a group of eighteen children who came from Poland in February, the little ones guided by a twelve-year-old child who had escaped from a German concentration camp. Money was needed to keep these little children in the home. I gave lecture recitals and gave the money to this home. The last sum I earned bought forty-five pairs of shoes before the Germans arrived.

In 1943, on January 5, my son was born. After three days he died. The day after he was born, one of the young doctors was in my room and said goodbye to me because he had to go to a labor camp that very night. I never saw him again. The day after the funeral a friend called to say that I should come home as my husband was in danger. He was being questioned by the counterespionage police because somebody had denounced him, saying that he had a secret radio station at his home. As a result, he had had a slight heart attack. Our cook ran out excitedly into the street and told this friend about the visit by the police, who then called me. I went home immediately. When I reached home I found our apartment in complete disorder, everything thrown on the floor and disheveled, and my husband ill. The cook told me that the questioning had been rough. Imre never told me anything more about it.

After this Imre slowed down more in his laboratory work. He now felt that as he had suffered a heart attack, he could not go to work every day. I resumed my house concerts and choir work. I never knew from one Monday to the next how many people would be able to attend. The labor camps were working to full capacity and I had no way of knowing who would be left by the next Monday evening's concert. The choir originally consisted of sixty people. By the end of the war there were only twelve. All the others were killed by the Germans or the Arrow Cross.

This sort of life continued until the Germans arrived on March 19, 1944. A few weeks before the German occupation everyone was told that they had to accept soldiers to be quartered in their houses and apartments. A general of the Hungarian gendarmerie came to our apartment house and went from apartment to apartment. Everybody gave some excuse why they could not let him stay in their apartment, saying, "you don't want to sleep here because the children are too noisy" or "you would be too uncomfortable in our apartment," and so on. But my husband and I looked into his eyes, decided that he looked like a decent human being, and told him that we had four rooms and there were only two of us so we could let him stay with us. I stipulated, however, that he could stay only if he liked music because I played the piano at irregular hours and once a week held a concert for Jewish refugees. I asked him if he thought he could survive this. He replied, "If you would be ashamed of me I can go to a hotel but if you would be kind enough to permit me I would like very much to stay here." Then he went on to look at some other apartments but in a half an hour he was back and told me that we were the only family who would accept him. He said, "I realize that I would inconvenience you so I have decided that I had better go to a hotel, but I would like to visit you from time to time." Then in about an hour he returned once again to say that since he was alone—his wife and little son were not in the city with him—he felt very lonely and would like to stay with us after all since he liked to be a part of a family.

It was strictly forbidden to listen to British and American broadcasts, but we always listened. The first evening the general was with us he, too, came in and listened with us. We took the risk and allowed him to do so. My husband said that we should always try to educate people. We never had enough food at this time and so it became the habit of the general to bring home some food every evening, which he must have taken from the kitchen of the gendarmerie.

The Sunday morning when the Germans occupied Hungary he was in the house. We were anxiously waiting to find out what effect the new situation would have upon him. We were afraid that he would undergo a complete change. We had already experienced this change in people from good to bad so often that we were prepared and would not have been surprised. When he came in he said, "Would you permit me to bring my wife and child here to stay with you? They will arrive tomorrow." We thought that he wanted to take over our apartment for his own family. However, when the wife and child arrived he introduced us to them in the following way: "If I do not survive the war or meet with some accident you must remember that this couple is a second family to me and you must defend and protect them." After the war we did everything possible to locate him so that we might act as character witnesses for this fine person, but we failed. He was probably killed by the Russians or by the Hungarian communists.

Soon after the Germans' arrival the bombing of Budapest started. The air raid shelter of our apartment house was its cellar. Since it was a large apartment house, as many as four hundred people often congregated in our cellar. We sat there on benches. Among us was one of the well-known Hungarian Nazis, Dr. Csik, a physician, who was later responsible for the extermination of 80 percent of the Jewish physicians. They did not know in the house that Imre and I did not have 100 percent "clean blood." At one of the first air raids the general sat with us on our bench. Dr. Csik and some of the other Nazis came over and invited him to sit with them. He said, "No, I am sitting with my new family."

My husband used these hours of inactivity to study physics, by the light of the little candles placed here and there about the basement.

4

The iron fist closes

From the day the Germans arrived it was forbidden for Imre to enter his laboratory as he was classified "unreliable," but he did go in for a few hours every day. One day three weeks later I received a sudden telephone call from Imre's secretary, saying, "You must disappear immediately."

I knew what this meant. Imre and I had prepared a code between us in case of emergency. However, it was hard for me to "disappear" immediately for I had with me a pupil, twelve years old, who was slightly subnormal. I tried hastily to leave, saying, "Listen, I have to go away now, we can't continue the lesson." He asked, "Why?" I replied that I could not tell him but I must leave immediately. Stubbornly, he stood his ground, saying, "I won't move until you tell me why." So I finally told him, half hysterically, "I must leave, the Gestapo are coming here, and if you don't go I will have to throw you out." Then he smiled and asked, "And you are going now to a hiding place?"

All this delay made me feel like screaming, but at last he went out and down the stairs, and I went down another stairway. As I went down I saw through the open iron grillwork in the elevator three Gestapo men coming up. I hurried down one flight of stairs and into the office of a woman doctor who lived directly below us and whom I knew slightly. Rushing in I told her, trembling, that the Gestapo were hunting for me. This kind woman immediately handed over a white coat to me just like the one she was wearing, saying quietly, "Now you are my assistant." Then as we waited we heard footsteps in the hallway above. We heard the doorbell to our apartment ring several times and then the sound of footsteps going away. Just before I left our apartment I had grabbed two jars belonging to my husband. One contained some stuff that was very important in an experiment he was conducting; the other contained some melted platinum. That was the form in which we kept all of our savings. I did not tell the lady physician what was in the jars, but I left them with her and said, "Please save these for us." Then I sneaked out of the house. I did not even have a coat on, but I was afraid to go back to our apartment. I thought, "I shall never return there." I racked my brain, trying to think where to go to be safe for a while. I had to go to somebody who never visited us, to someone whom the janitor in our building had never seen (janitors in Budapest were the great spying eyes and seemed to know everyone even slightly connected with all tenants). Finally, I hit upon the idea to go to my psychoanalyst. I had not gone far when I ran into Imre's secretary, who had called me on the phone. She told me what had led to her call.

Before Imre arrived in the laboratory, three Gestapo men had come in and said that they had received reports that Dr. Patai had a secret radio station and that he was guilty of sabotage and various other crimes, so they would have to conduct a search. A physicist colleague and friend of my husband, Dr. John Kudar, to whom I shall always be grateful, was present at the time. He, himself, was not "guilty" of the crime of having a grandmother of Jewish blood. He spoke to the Gestapo men and told them that my husband was a good Hungarian and a fine scientist, and put up as good a case as he possibly could in Imre's defense. He ended by saying that he knew that Imre never participated in any sabotage.

When Dr. Kudar finished speaking, they inquired, "When will he come in?" He told them that Imre would probably be in in an hour. They left, saying they would be back. While

Dr. Kudar was talking to the Gestapo, he saw out of the corner of his eye Imre coming up the street toward the building. He excused himself for a moment, went out of the room, and told the secretary to run out and warn Imre not to come in. She did this. There was a bench in front of the laboratory, and Imre sat down there and waited until the three men left. Then he went in and Dr. Kudar said, "Go away and don't come back." Imre stood and thought for a little while. Then he told his friend, "I will stay and meet them because I cannot expose my family and my wife's family to their retribution." Imre then asked the secretary to go out and call me and tell me that I must disappear. Later he asked her to try to find me because he was worried that in my excitement I would hide in some friend's or neighbor's apartment where it would be easy to find me. This is how I ran into her as I left the house.

Imre stayed in the laboratory. After about an hour the three Gestapo men came back and found him there. They searched the laboratory. About the only thing they could find was the little quartz lamp. This looked suspicious because it had to be heated with high frequency waves. They jumped to the conclusion that it was some sort of radio instrument. When they accused Imre of this he explained to them the function of the lamp, and suggested that he could demonstrate its function if one of them was willing to swallow it. None of them was a big enough hero to accept the suggestion. Imre was a psychologist, so he set about trying to turn this search into a discussion in a purely scientific direction. He knew that Germans were trained in school in a very thorough way, and he thought that by explaining to them in an interesting way the different research problems he was working on he would divert their attention from their grim mission and put them into a better frame of mind. He succeeded in doing this, especially with one of them who became quite friendly. He was the leader of the group, named Graef. (This man later played a very important role in our lives.) Finally, he said, "Let's go to your home now. We should like to see your wife and search the place."

Imre answered that I was probably out teaching somewhere since I did not teach at home. They said that they received just the opposite impression. When they went upstairs to our apartment, they met a boy coming down. They questioned him and found out that he was my pupil. They asked him where Mrs. Patai was and he said that I ran out in a hurry because I received a telephone call that the Gestapo was coming. The boy even told them that I did not finish my lesson and was on my way to a hiding place. Imre was, of course, quite embarrassed, but he somehow talked himself out of the situation. He said that the boy they saw was not quite normal and had invented the whole thing. This did not sound so bad because, as I said before, the boy was actually subnormal, and doubtless the Gestapo men could see that when they talked to him.

Before Imre and the others had started to go to our apartment, he excused himself for a moment and left a second message with the secretary that if I could be located I should go home. This succeeded, and I started home. Meanwhile, the three men made a thorough search of the apartment and found nothing. Or, more correctly, they did find a black lamp that Imre used for examination of food and various other tests. They asked him what that was for. Imre held up the lamp to the face of one of them and said, "You have a gold-filled tooth in your upper jaw on the right side." He did something similar with the other man. Both men were completely fascinated. It sounded like Sherlock Holmes to them. Just about that time I arrived home. As I opened the door to the apartment Imre came over to me and told me to come in and not to be afraid, that these men would not harm us. He introduced us and we talked for a little while. The men then said they were leaving but that Imre should come down to headquarters early next morning. This meant that they were giving us a night in which to escape.

Imre and I stayed up all night trying to decide what to do. We decided to talk to the general staying with us and see what he advised. Imre felt that it would not be good psychologically if we talked to him while he was in uniform, so we waited until he had his bath and put on his bathrobe, and then we approached him. He listened to our story, sitting with us for hours in this informal attire. At the end he told us that he was our friend, that his sympathy was completely with us, but that this was a situation in which he was unable to advise us. Whichever way we decided, it may turn out wrong. The upshot of it was that Imre made up his mind that he would not try to escape, but would go to head-quarters in the morning. The general said that it was one of the bravest things he had ever heard.

Early the next morning Imre left our apartment and went to the Gestapo headquarters. Before he left he took off his wedding ring and his watch and gave them to me. There was a very gentle little smile on his face as he handed them over and said, "I don't need these for the hearings." He knew—and I knew—that practically no one ever came back from the "hearings." Some friends from the laboratory went along with him as witnesses, and witnesses were very much needed. When he left I also went out to find some additional help for him. I went first to a so-called friend who, instead of helping me, said, "You should go to the Gestapo yourself and tell Imre that he should cooperate with the Germans in the future." Naturally, I did not do this. Then I went to another man, a very important person, who could have helped if he wanted to. When I begged him to get Imre out he flatly refused, saying, "I never interfere in such matters." Finally, I went to my husband's patent lawyer who was also a close friend of ours. He knew that he could not do anything, but he tried to keep me in his office as long as possible. He knew that all hopes were futile, but by talking to me he tried to divert my attention and keep me from going insane.

After many hours I received a call from Dr. Kudar, who went with Imre as one of his witnesses. He asked me to come immediately to a café where he would meet me. I rushed there and found him sitting at a table with my husband. I do not have to tell how we both felt. Imre told me briefly about the hours he spent with the Gestapo. Part of it was very disagreeable—some of the officers did not treat him with gloved hands—but in the end Mr. Graef saved him. He was the man who reported Imre's case, and his conclusion was that Imre had not committed any acts of sabotage. Before they let Imre go, an incident happened that was difficult to understand. Mr. Graef asked him to come to his room. They were alone there. He pulled out a little radio tube and told Imre that it was from his own private set and it had burned out recently. He said, "I can't get another one like it. Would you be kind enough to get me a replacement?" It was a strange request. Here was Imre, his fate hanging on a narrow thread between life and death, and here was a powerful Gestapo officer, asking him the favor of getting a radio tube, which he probably could just as easily get himself. Imre said to me: "The whole business looks fishy. According to all the rules of the game, they should at least have put me in jail."

After three tense weeks, one morning at 6 o'clock the bell rang. Imre glanced at me and said, "Looks like the Gestapo is back." He went to the door and shouted, "Who is it?" The answer: "The political police." This was the Hungarian version of the Gestapo. Imre refused to open the door and demanded that the man show his identification card and state the charges against him. The man shouted back, "It will be much worse for you if you resist." I was very scared and opened the door. The man entered. We were both still in pajamas. He said to Imre: "Dress yourself and come with me." Imre replied: "All right, I will. But first please sit down and tell me what is this all about." The man sat down and said: "You have a laboratory; its name is IVACO. It means International Vacuum-Technical Company. The name is English. Your 'International' connection is with the British and the Americans. We know that you work for them. We have information that you have committed various acts of sabotage." Before Imre could answer a thought came to me in a flash, and I spoke first: "You are completely misinformed. The name IVACO means Imre's Vacuum-Technical Company. First he meant to call it AVACO, the A in it meaning Agi's. He wanted to name it after me, but I said I have nothing to do with science, you are the scientist, let us name it after you. So we named it IVACO." The man accepted this childish explanation.

Then he turned to Imre and continued: "The other charge against you is that you hired Jews to work in your laboratory. You know that is against the law." This accusation, like the other, was also true, but naturally Imre repudiated it. However, the denial did not avail much; the man insisted that Imre must come with him to headquarters. There was nothing else to do but to acquiesce, so Imre went into the bathroom to shave and dress himself. I was sitting alone in my pajamas with the Gestapo man. My thoughts ran very fast, and I tried to imagine how Imre would use his psychology to handle this man if he were in my place. I thought that if I could somehow establish a human contact with him, it would ease the tension and might help in some way Imre's desperate situation. For a minute or two I sat silently. Then I turned to the Gestapo man with a kind smile and said: "You have such an interesting and important profession." He was completely taken aback and answered: "It is a gangster's profession." I laughed inwardly; the contact was established, and I felt that I had the situation in hand. We started a conversation, and after a while he looked at me and said: "Do not be afraid. I will bring your husband home." Then I told him that my husband had had a heart attack and that I was terribly afraid of the hearing because I knew about the methods that were used in those hearings. He said that it was true that the man before whom Imre was supposed to appear was a very cruel, sadistic person, but he would see to it that Imre should not go before this man, and promised that he himself would conduct the hearing. I told Mr. Cserna, whose name I knew by this time, that Imre had already been questioned by the counter-espionage and the German Gestapo, and they acquitted him. Mr. Cserna then told me, "Go help your husband," and that gave me an opportunity to tell Imre what he had told me.

The two men left shortly after this and I was alone. I was by no means certain that Mr. Cserna would or could keep his promise. I waited in the apartment all day. I ate nothing and did nothing but sit at the window waiting for Imre. Finally, he returned in the late afternoon, looking exhausted. The hearing was not as gentle as was promised. I do not know any of the details, for Imre never related them to me, but he told me that he was taken out of the hands of our very kind man, against his protests, and handed over to somebody else.

That evening Imre suffered a very severe heart attack. It was a day of many air raids and I was unable to get a doctor. His attack lasted six hours before I could get one. He told me that Imre must be taken to a hospital immediately. To add to all our troubles, this was the day on which a new "Jewish law" became effective. According to this law, every person who had one-quarter or one-half or full Jewish blood in him had to sew on his clothing a yellow star, on the left side, just above the heart. Since our blood was not "clean," both Imre and I wore the yellow stars. It was almost impossible to get an ambulance or a hospital bed for yellow-star people at that time. Still, I finally succeeded in getting an ambulance and found a little private hospital that accepted both of us. I did not dare to stay at home alone.

The doctor examined Imre and told me that he had only a few hours to live, but the next day he felt much better—only his spirit was somewhat depressed. He asked the doctor whether they did any sort of medical research in that hospital. He knew that he was doomed to stay in bed for some days to come, and he said that he would like to help them with whatever research they were working on. He also told the doctor about his work on kidney stones. The doctor replied that there were several patients in the hospital who had kidney troubles. Imre begged him to bring some laboratory equipment into his room. When this request was granted and the equipment was brought in, Imre conducted several hundred experiments while lying in bed, testing the urine of people suffering from kidney problems. He also got a number of books from the university to read up on biochemistry. The doctor came to his room every evening around 8 o'clock, and worked with my deadly sick husband until 11 or 12 o'clock at night.

Several days later the order came that all persons wearing the yellow star must leave their homes and must move into the so-called "yellow-star houses." I told my husband that I would have to leave the hospital and look for a room in one of these yellow-star houses for us. The next day the head of the clinic called me into his office and showed me the morning paper. It stated that every engineer who wore the yellow star was to be deported to concentration camps in Germany, and every yellow-star woman under forty would be ordered into a labor camp. He then told me that Imre would die immediately if he were moved, and added that I should not tell him this but should do everything I could to save the life of such a man.

The first thing that occurred to me was to go to the doctor who worked with my husband on the kidneys from the time Imre came to the hospital. I told him that I did not know what his views were about the things going on around us, but I had great confidence in him, and if he could help us it would mean everything to me. He answered that for the past two days he had been expecting a patient of his to die who had an incurable disease. He would be willing to steal the documents of this man after he died and give them to Imre. When Imre recovered, probably in several weeks, he could be released from the hospital with the dead man's papers. He finished by saying: "If you love your husband so much, pray that this patient will not linger on but will die very soon."

But our time was running out, and I could not wait for the man to die. In desperation my thoughts turned to Mr. Graef, the kind Gestapo man who had saved Imre's life. I felt that he must be a good man, so I decided to play my last card and ask his help. I called the German Gestapo and said that I would like to speak to Mr. Graef. A man came to the phone, and answered it. I tried to put into my voice all the friendly confidence I had in him, and said to him: "Mr. Graef, I am Mrs. Patai. You doubtless remember my husband and me. We need your help. Would you be kind enough to visit us in our apartment?" This was our last day in the apartment; the next day we were to move into the yellow-star house.

The voice at the other end of the line answered in a very gruff tone, "No, I don't remember you at all." I was terribly disappointed but did not give up, and said, "I have the radio tube for you." This was not true, but I had to find some way of baiting him so that I might have a chance to plead our case. He said, "What radio tube?" I saw that I was getting nowhere fast, so I said, "Look, I must see you. I have something very important to tell you." He replied, "All right, tell me right now." I said, "I can't. It is very personal. I cannot tell it to you over the phone." So finally he consented and said, "I will be at your apartment at 5 o'clock sharp." I left the hospital, telling Imre that I was going out to find a room for us in a yellow-star house. I also told his doctor that if I did not return I would probably be dead, and the cause of it would be a German Gestapo man named Graef.

I arrived at our apartment a few minutes before five. At exactly 5 o'clock someone rang the doorbell. I opened the door and in came a man over six feet tall, with dark hair, very thin, and wearing the uniform of a high officer of the Gestapo. Mr. Graef was a short, stout man, with very blond hair, and kind blue eyes. My visitor shouted at me, "What do you want from me?" I replied, "But you are not Mr. Graef." He said, "No, my name is Graes." I felt I was lost. This ironic stroke of fate would probably cause me to lose my one last hope for help. Tears of disappointment filled my eyes as I stammered, "But I wanted Mr. Graef." In his loud, coarse voice he demanded rudely, "What did you want from Mr. Graef?" I did not answer, so he repeated his question more threateningly. Then in my distress I said the only thing that came into my mind: "I hope that you are enough of a gentleman not to ask why a lady asks a gentleman to her apartment, when she is obviously alone." This unexpected answer had its effect, and he backed out, muttering "I am sorry, I will send Mr. Graef to you."

As soon as he left, I rushed to the telephone, called the Gestapo, and asked for Mr. Graef. This time it was really Mr. Graef who came to the phone. He recognized me immediately and said that he would be over in half an hour. In exactly half an hour my second Gestapo guest arrived and started with the same question, except this time it was spoken more politely, "Why did you ask me to come over?" I answered in my most innocent voice, "Please will you give us some false papers? Otherwise my husband will be deported and I shall have to go into a labor camp." He looked at me as though he could not believe he had heard me correctly, then said, "Mrs. Patai, you are either very brave or very stupid to ask such a thing from a Gestapo officer." I answered, "Mr. Graef, you are also either very brave or very stupid, having done what you have already done for my husband. When you had to take him to your headquarters, you told me not to be afraid, that you would save him. Your kindness even went so far that you falsified some of the witnesses' statements in his favor. I could go to the Gestapo now and tell them all this." He looked at me quizzically, then began to smile, and said, "Mrs. Patai, you are as good a psychologist as your husband. The way he was able to tame my two associates was really remarkable, and the way you are handling this situation is just as good." He continued, telling me that he had no way of giving us false papers, but that he had a car and could help us to escape to Prague. In Warsaw, where he had been stationed before, he had helped many people escape. He had such great respect for my husband that he was willing to do everything in his power to save him. The trip to Prague would have to wait a while because he was a newcomer in Hungary and had not yet familiarized himself with the unwatched roads. This was indispensable, since the trip would have to be made in darkness. He added that there was no immediate urgency for the trip because the order for the deportation of engineers would be postponed. The Nazis had come to the conclusion that at this stage the engineers were still needed. He told me also that I should notify him of our future address as soon as I found a room in a yellow-star house. He left, reaffirming that I could count on him. He did not accept any drink, cigarettes, or money. I asked him how much the trip to Prague would cost, and he said it would cost nothing. The only jarring note was that he inquired about the radio tube. I still could not understand why he could not order it through the Gestapo.

Before I left the apartment, the janitor told me that the Hungarian political police had come on the day we went to the hospital and inquired what had happened to Dr. Patai. Naturally, this did not make me feel any better. It gave the crowning touch to the events of that nightmarish evening.

5

Life in a yellow-star house

After much searching I found a room in one of the apartments of a yellow-star house. There were already twenty-three people living in that apartment. The reason that I took this place was that our family physician and his wife had a room there, and I felt that Imre would be safer near a doctor after his two heart attacks. The wearers of the yellow star were permitted to take with them enough furniture for one room. Before the move, the janitor came to me and said, "Mrs. Patai, you'd better give me your belongings, otherwise I will take them, anyhow. You will not need them; you will be killed sooner or later." Then without waiting he proceeded to help himself to our belongings, starting with the clothes of our baby who died. I called up two men who had worked in Imre's factory to help me pack, and they also helped themselves generously to whatever they wanted of our things.

I chose Imre's books, my piano, two beds, a table, and some chairs. These were put on a horse-drawn wagon. A friend of mine, also a yellow-star woman, and I sat with the driver in the front seat. As we moved slowly on our way to the yellow-star house, we saw endless rows of wagons like ours winding through the streets of Budapest. The city had about 200,000 Jews, and those who were still alive, and not in labor camps, were now moving into the yellow-star houses. My friend looked at me and

31

said, "This is our last free removal." As the wagon creaked along the children on the streets—and some adults too—threw dirt into our faces.

Imre, of course, knew nothing about what was going on in the outside world. He was busy with the experiments in his hospital room. But soon reality caught up with him. A small building in the hospital, which stood very close to the one in which we were staying, was completely demolished by a direct hit from a bomb. The head of one of the nurses and the leg of a doctor flew in through Imre's window on the second floor—not a soothing sight for a patient recovering from a heart attack. Our hospital building was also damaged, so that we had no light, water, or gas, and all the windows were blown out. Imre's doctor advised us to leave the hospital, so we moved into our new home in the yellow-star house.

No sooner had we arrived than an air raid started, and Imre had to get from the fourth floor to the cellar as fast as he could. Most of the air raid shelters were forbidden to yellow-star people, and the few that were left to us were jammed so tightly that there was no room to breathe. In such surroundings Imre's life was in danger. But, fortunately for all of us, his ingenuity did not leave him. After fumbling around in the darkness, he found a hidden passage between the "yellow cellar" and the "Aryan cellar." I brought down two easy chairs and two straight-backed chairs, and afterward here in this secluded corner twenty or more people frequently stayed for hours and hours during air raids.

It was July 1944. Our family doctor had just been released from jail after suffering a nervous breakdown. He had tried to save the life of a child who came from Czechoslovakia as a refugee, by hiding the child in his home. His cook had informed on him to the police and he was thrown into jail. After his release he suffered from severe depression. Imre made it his job to try to save him from breakdown. I had chosen this particular yellow-star house because I wanted my husband to be near his physician, and now he was near him but with the roles exchanged. Imre sat many long hours of the day and night at the bedside of our doctor and friend. Gradually, he brought him back so that he again became interested in research, reading, and discussion.

Life moved slowly in our yellow-star prison. The doors of the house were locked, and only once in a while were we permitted to leave the house for an hour. We had a phone in our room, so we had a means of communication with the outside world. Phones were not permitted in yellow-star houses except for physicians, but we had two physicians in our house. Our food ration cards were yellow, which meant that we had practically nothing to eat. But we had a butler. His job was to keep in order an apartment in which twenty-five people lived. He had volunteered to do this job. We had no money to pay him; all we could give him was a little food and a corner in which to sleep.

Imre worked out a plan to keep up a spiritual life in the house. Every afternoon the young people came into our room, and he taught them physics, psychology, literature, and other subjects. There was a psychoanalyst in the house, too, with whom Imre had many interesting discussions. The other physician in the house came to Imre every day to discuss with him his ideas on the curing of rheumatism. In addition, Imre insisted that I should play every other evening for as many people as we could manage to crowd into the apartment.

One day the political police showed up in our midst again. It was the same kind Mr. Cserna about whom I have spoken before (the man who said that his job was a gangster's job). He told me that soon after Imre's hearing he tried to visit us in our old home, and then he found that Imre was in hospital. Ever since, he had been suffering from a bad conscience, because he felt that he was partly responsible for Imre's illness. The reason he came now was to warn us that we were again in danger and to offer us his help. He had a sweetheart, a Jewish girl, who was an expert at forging false papers, and many of the people whom Mr. Cserna had been ordered to arrest were saved by the skill of his lady-love. He promised us that the lady would come to visit us the following day and would give us false papers.

Sure enough, the next day Mr. Cserna's girlfriend arrived. Her name was Sarika (I do not remember her last name). She gave us blank identification papers that we could fill out ourselves. They cost us nothing, which was fortunate, because just a few days before Imre bought me a set of false papers for a thousand pengős, which was practically all the money we had. (I shall tell about these papers later.) Sarika was working for the Swedish Red Cross. She also had some connections with the Hungarian Army Staff—a general or a colonel was a friend of hers. She hinted that she could get some military secrets for us. I suppose she thought that we belonged to the underground where such information would be of great value.

Shortly after this visit, one morning the Hungarian Counterespionage Police appeared at our door. This may be a little confusing, but the agents of three different secret service organizations were on Imre's trail: the German Gestapo, the Hungarian Political Police, and the Hungarian Counterespionage Police. This time, three counterespionage agents came and took my husband away. He was gone for about twenty-four hours, and he came home in a very bad condition. The next morning at 6:30 the same three men were back again to question me. They asked me where Imre kept his instruments, his books, his notes; they asked me about his business connections, his friends, and so forth. They saw on my piano my pocket metronome, and immediately declared that it was a part of a time bomb. Of course, they knew better, but this gave them an opportunity to steal my metronome. Next they came across my diaries, which I had kept since I was eleven years old. They read them at great length, hoping to find some incriminating evidence against me. They read with glee the story of my first love—at the age of eleven—while I burned with anger and embarrassment. Finally, they seemed to have found something that gave them a foothold. On one page they came across a sentence that I must have written when I was about fifteen. It read: "If I do decide to make a career of my music, and if I make a success of it, I will not spend my money, like many artists, on jewelry and dresses, but I am going to help other artists." They declared that this was a communistic idea, and I must go with them to their headquarters. Incidentally, the whole questioning was not as quiet as it sounds now; quite a bit of our furniture got broken in the process.

While this was going on, part of the time Imre was in our room, and part of the time he was taken to another room for separate questioning. Then, just at the moment when the three agents decided that they had enough evidence to take me along, a miracle happened. The air raid sirens began to shriek and American bombers appeared over Budapest. At that moment an intuitive thought flashed through my mind. I felt—for the first time—that America would be our fate, our salvation, our future.

The bombs began to fall, and the three heroes of the Hungarian Counterespionage Police ran for shelter. Before they left, they assured us that they would be back for me right after the air raid. But Imre and I did not wait for their return. We rushed out from the house, and in the midst of one of the severest bombings, ran to the home of a friend. Imre and I had once saved the life of this man. We begged him to keep us for one night. The next minute we were on the street again, because he had kicked us out. We wandered around the whole afternoon until a man connected with the Portuguese Legation took us into his home. He had been a member of my choir. He and his wife accepted us with open arms.

We spent a week with them in peace. During the day we kept to our beds; at night we came out and discussed music, literature, and philosophy with our host and hostess. Imre said with a cheerful grin that this had been the first restful week of his life. We sent a message to our butler in the yellow-star house, and he came to us faithfully every day, bringing food and newspapers. He also contacted Mr. Cserna, who came to visit us. He promised us that he would intercede with the Hungarian Counterespionage Police, and would assure them that the Hungarian Political Police would handle our case—which meant him. At the end of the week he notified us that we could go home. He had arranged the matter with the Hungarian Counterespionage Police, and nobody would bother us.

Soon after our return we began our career in the Hungarian underground movement. One day a gentleman came to call on a lady who lived in our "community apartment." We were introduced to each other and started talking about a number of things. Imre and I liked him immediately. Later he came into our room and said: "You are like a herd of cattle destined for the slaughterhouse, waiting patiently for the axe." "It is true, but what else can we do?" I replied. "You can fight back," was his answer. Then he proceeded to explain that with various acts of sabotage we could help to disorganize the activities of the Germans and the Arrow Cross. We could throw nails on the streets to puncture the tires of German trucks. We could spread gasoline about in the attics of houses to start fires at an opportune moment. Our spontaneous reaction was, "We will do it." We had never thought before of doing such bad-boy acts, but at that time it seemed like a good idea. Perhaps such little things—if done by many—would mount up.

The next day Imre managed to get fifteen pounds of nails. During the air raids and at night, Imre, the butler, and I sneaked out of the house and threw them onto the streets. Imre hammered some into the tires of parked cars and trucks. We got hold of cans of gasoline and placed them in the attics of thirty houses. Unfortunately, we had access only to yellow-star houses, but the idea was that if the order for general deportation of the yellow-star people came out, these fires might be started. It would create a tremendous confusion, and the inhabitants could utilize it to escape and go into hiding.

A week later the same gentleman returned and asked us whether we had followed his suggestions. We told him what we did, and he was very pleased He then revealed that he was one of the organizers of the underground movement, the head of which was Professor Szent-Györgyi. He confessed that he had wanted only to try us out and test our loyalty, and did not really want us to start fires. He wanted to see whether the Patai couple would obey orders and demonstrate their suitability for underground work. He ended by asking us whether we would be willing to join up. We replied with an enthusiastic yes.

This was in August 1944. Imre was immediately assigned a technical job. The underground had three broadcasting stations, and one of them was out of order. They could not determine what was wrong, but Imre found the trouble and put the station back into operation. Soon Imre had a plan of his own that, however, was unfortunately not accepted. It was well known that the eight bridges of Budapest had been mined by the Germans. Imre worked out how to disconnect the mines, so that if the Germans tried to blow up the bridges they would fail. He offered to carry out the plan himself, at the risk of his life. The leader of our group refused the offer. He was an optimist, and he felt that the Germans would not blow up the bridges in any case. Imre was very unhappy over this Pollyannaish attitude, but there was nothing he could do; he had to obey orders.

My assignment was of a very different nature. I was to make preparations for the situation following the liberation from the Nazis. My job was to find reliable people who could replace the Nazis later in responsible positions, mostly in the field of music and the arts. These people had to be trustworthy enough to work with the underground during the remainder of the war, and capable enough to handle important jobs after the war. Gradually, I built up a card index of 400 people—and it was not easy. I built it up in a snowball fashion, starting with people I knew and continuing with others recommended by them. I contacted everyone in person, using every opportunity I had to slip out of the yellow-star house, meeting them secretly on street corners, in restaurants, in their apartments, and so forth. It was a dangerous work, but I was very happy doing it.

In this period Sarika, Mr. Cserna's girlfriend, visited us frequently. Late one night she came to us with an exciting story. That morning she had been in the Ministry of War, having some business with her friend, the general, when two senior German officers arrived from Bucharest. The general happened to be very busy, so he asked Sarika to entertain the distinguished visitors. They went sightseeing, they had a number of drinks, and gradually the two gentlemen became very talkative. They told her that their mission was to take the gold reserves of Romania and deliver it to the Royal Palace in Buda, where it would be deposited until the end of the war. Sarika started to flirt with the officers and went with them to their hotel, where I expect they had some more drinks. One of the officers actually opened a huge suitcase and showed her that it was full of gold. The time of delivery to the palace was to be 9 o'clock the next morning.

Imre and I did not know whether to believe Sarika's story or not, but to be on the safe side Imre immediately left to contact the underground. The leaders decided to stage a hold-up. They felt that if the gold could be taken and kept until the end of the war, and then returned to Romania, it would make a good impression on the Allies and would help Hungary in the peace negotiations. However, the plan failed. Maybe the German officers realized how foolish they were to prattle so freely. At any rate, they left an hour earlier and the hold-up party saw them only on their way back from the Palace, without any luggage. Of course, it is possible that Sarika invented the gold story—although ordinarily the information she supplied us was pretty reliable.

For example, on another occasion she told us that she had found out from her general friend that the main ammunition reserves of the Hungarian Army were located in a small street in Pest, and she named the street. Imre immediately contacted the underground, and Sarika's story was verified. Two days later the leader of our group came to us and asked whether we had any friends living in that street. He wanted to warn them to move away, because the underground had decided to blow up the ammunition. We did not have any friends in that street. A few days later, the little street with every house in it was completely demolished.

I should like to add here parenthetically that the reason why I do not want to name the leader of our underground group is that he is still living in Hungary. It is no merit these days that somebody had risked his life to fight the Nazis. On the contrary, it is a crime. Those who had the courage to fight the Nazis may still have some courage left to fight the communists.

6

Close to insanity

It happened around this time that I narrowly escaped deportation on two successive days. A doctor friend of ours visited us, under some pretext, one afternoon in the yellow-star house. He was not a yellow-star person himself—he had clean blood. Suddenly, a group of Hungarian soldiers marched into the house intending to take every woman under forty to concentration camps. Two of the soldiers came into our room to take me. The doctor said to them: "This lady is my nurse. She came with me." They looked somewhat dubious, so he slipped some money into their hands. That convinced them, and they left. But next day they came back to attend to the remaining women. We had to go out into the courtyard where we were lined up and listed for the deportation. I was standing next to a very dear friend of mine. She whispered into my ear: "Go upstairs, you must not come with us."

I whispered back: "I do not dare." She said: "For God's sake, go immediately or I shall do something desperate." I stepped out of the line, went up to one of the soldiers, and said: "I must go to the toilet." At the same time I put some money into his hand. He said: "Go ahead." I rushed into one of the apartments, locked myself in the bathroom, and waited. It was a long wait—but no one came for me. The money did it. After a while the women in the courtyard were driven away, on the long road to a German concentration camp. Not a single one returned.

It is hard to see now what kept us from going insane in those days. One day Imre told me that someone had committed suicide in the house. We began to talk about the epidemic of suicides in Holland that we had witnessed after the Nazi invasion, and we felt that we must do something to prevent such an epidemic here. During a sleepless night I concocted a crazy idea, at least it seems crazy now in retrospect, though at that time it had a semblance of sanity and even feasibility.

I got up, dressed, removed my yellow star, and sneaked out of the house. I went back to the apartment house where we lived before, to pay a visit to our former neighbor, Dr. Laezlo Csik. I mentioned his name already in my story. He was the head of the Hungarian Medical Association and the most dangerous Nazi bloodhound in Hungary. I was the only person in his waiting room, and in five minutes I was admitted into his office. Apparently, he did not know that we had had to move out of the apartment house, because he greeted me by saying, "Oh, I have not heard you play the piano for such a long time." I answered: "You haven't heard my playing because you kicked us out of our home." He said he did not understand. I said: "I am a yellow-star woman, I had to move into a yellow-star house. I want to talk with you, and because I could not come to you wearing my yellow star I took it off. You can call the police and report me." Taken aback by this smiling introduction to the conversation, he asked: "What can I do for you? Are you ill?" "No, Dr. Csik," I replied, "I am not ill. I want to tell you something. Hungary is a big hunting ground today. Some people hunt and murder, others are hunted and killed. I am a yellow-star woman, I do not belong to the group of murderers. You do not wear the yellow star, you are a Nazi leader, you know which group you belong to. When you received your medical degree you took an oath that binds you to the highest moral principles, an oath that binds you to help those who are in need. Let us look into each other's eyes, the murderer and the victim, and give me an honest answer. No one can hear us. Why do you murder us?"

He listened calmly to my impassioned speech and did not delay with his answer. "For two thousand years the people of Aryan blood have been enslaved by the Jews. But now Heaven sent us a great leader, Adolph Hitler, to liberate us from our chains. Your time is up. This is the day of our great revenge. We can kill and we will kill everyone who is in our way. We do not care whether it is a newborn baby or a sick, old woman. We do not care whether he is innocent or guilty. We must give an outlet to our hatred."

I felt sick at heart, trembling all over, but I tried to hold myself together and to talk sensibly. I pointed out to him that he could not have been suppressed so badly by the Jews since he had been the head of the medical association for many years, and he was known to be one of the wealthiest doctors in the country. Then I came to the main point of my visit. I told him that I had a plan that I believed was reasonable. I said: "Let my husband and I, and others, organize the yellow-star people into a camp. At the end of the war, if we lose the war, we promise that we shall leave the country. If you lose the war, we promise we shall save you for saving so many innocent souls." He answered: "Do not worry about our fate after the war, lady. We have a good alibi. We are under German occupation. If we lose the war, we can say that the Germans forced us to do what we did." I replied: "You may say it, but some of your victims will survive and will tell the truth." Dr. Csik smiled sardonically: "My dear lady, you will all die. But you are a very interesting person. If you do survive, visit me after the war."

I could not stand it any longer. I turned and left his office, slamming the door behind me. Then I ran home as fast as I could and told Imre about my visit with Dr. Csik. We both felt that there was not much hope left for us and our kind.

That same night I called up Mr. Graef at the Gestapo and denounced Dr. Csik to him. I told him what Dr. Csik had said to me about using the Germans as an alibi for the activities of the Arrow Cross if they lost the war. It was a strange situation to denounce a Nazi bloodhound to a Gestapo officer. A week later we read in a newspaper that Dr. Csik was in disgrace. I have no idea what part my denunciation played in this.

Before I leave the subject of Dr. Csik, I should like to mention one more incident briefly to show what sort of a man he was. A few weeks after my visit he entered a sanatorium in Budapest, leading a group of Arrow Cross hoodlums, and demanded to know whether there were any persons of Jewish blood there. There was a Jewish woman in the sanatorium on whom they had just performed a Caesarian operation. The Nazis threw the woman and the newborn baby out into the street where both died. I heard this story from one of the doctors of that sanatorium. This was one of the more *innocent* acts of Dr. Csik.

7

A remarkable Gestapo officer

In 1944 our main protector next to God was the Gestapo officer Mr. Graef. One afternoon he visited us and showed us a document with the following text: "Dr. Imre Patai, well-known international scientist faker, intends to leave the country together with his wife, Agi Jambor. The proof of their intentions is that Dr. Patai has already grown a moustache and Mrs. Patai has dyed her hair blond."

Now I have to go back a little to explain the situation. I mentioned that sometime previously Imre bought for me a set of false papers. It consisted of a birth certificate, a marriage certificate, and two workbooks—two because this particular woman had two professions. One of her jobs was in a laundry, sorting clothes, and the other was more lucrative—she was a prostitute. Her name was Maria Kocsmáros. Her husband, John, had been killed in the war, so she was entitled to a small monthly army widow's pension. The purchase price of the papers included the right to draw her pension, but I never used this right.

When we bought these papers, we naturally hoped that I would never have to use them. For quite a while I did not assume the identity of Maria Kocsmáros, but eventually it became necessary to do so. Since the papers of Maria stated that she had blond hair, I did bleach my hair blond. Maria also had blue eyes, and on this point I was stuck. I could not change the color of my eyes, so we changed the papers instead to "brown eyes." As you remember, perhaps, we had also received some blank identification papers from Sarika. These papers were still blank, for we had not settled yet on Imre's new identity, but we had decided that the new Imre must have a moustache. So he grew one.

The paper that Mr. Graef showed us also stated that the Patais were dangerous individuals, that we had good connections with foreign legations, and that all border stations should he alerted for our possible escape. Then Mr. Graef turned the paper over and pointed to what he had written on the reverse side: "Visited the family. They do not intend to escape. All future denunciations should be treated as lies." He looked at me gently and said: "Didn't I visit the family?" And he added that since he did not know how long he would live, he was leaving this paper in his desk so that his successor would also know that the Patai case had been taken care of.

On another occasion he came to us in the middle of the night and told us to contact all of our friends because within a week the general deportation of all Jews, or more correctly all yellow-star people, would begin in Budapest. Imre made all the contacts he could, but four days later Mr. Graef came again and said that the order will not be issued after all. The Nazi high command decided that slave workers were still needed in Hungary.

In one of our conversations with Mr. Graef, the mystery of the radio tube was also clarified. Imre once gathered up his courage and asked him why he wanted that radio tube. He confessed that he had a private radio set of his own that he used to listen secretly to the British broadcasts. Naturally, when the tube went bad he could not ask the Gestapo to replace it. We also learned from him gradually the story of his life and of his family. We knew that he had a little son who was a child prodigy on the piano. In appreciation for saving our lives so many times I offered to give him our piano, but he refused.

One day, during the hour we were permitted to leave the house, the Hungarian Counterespionage Police again made its appearance. Our butler—and friend, and fellow member in the underground—told us that they first inquired after my husband. He told them that Dr. Patai was not at home. "Then we shall take his wife," they replied. "She is not at home, either." "We shall take their child then." "They have no children." "All right then, we shall be back." Imre looked at me sadly and said, "Looks as though we'll have to face it again." But I replied, "You're crazy, you cannot stay here." And I convinced him that we should both escape. We left the house and went to the office of a friend of ours, the obstetrician who had delivered our child. There I left Imre and went into a public telephone booth to call Mr. Graef. I asked him to come over immediately in his official yellow car. He said he could not come because he had to inspect a prison. I insisted: "Nothing is as important now as meeting me."

In ten minutes I met him on the street and got into his car. I told him that he would have to arrest us officially in order to protect us from the Hungarian Counterespionage Police. He answered that he could not do that because if he were killed the next day, we would find ourselves in the position of being really under arrest, and that would be the end of us. I realized that this was true. I suggested, therefore, that he should make at least a sham arrest, so that people should believe that we were in the hands of the Gestapo. He agreed to this, and we went back to the yellow-star house. He called out our Nazi janitor and told him: "This woman tells me that her husband is not in the house. I want to arrest both of them for working against the Germans. I will search the house. The woman will come with me." The two of us then went through the house searching for Imre, who was in the office of our obstetrician friend.

When Mr. Graef searched our room, he raised his voice so that everyone in the apartment could hear it: "You can take some of your things with you." He stuffed his own pockets full of things that I was not able to carry myself. Then he wrote an official notice of arrest that read: "To All Official Authorities: I hereby arrest Dr. and Mrs. Imre Patai for anti-German activities. All interested in further information regarding them should contact the undersigned.

H. Graef, Geheime Staatspolizei." He gave this notice to the janitor, saying, "I am certain that other official authorities will also try to find these people. Send them to me at the Gestapo." We went out. He took me back to the obstetrician, embraced me, and said: "Now you are free." He promised me that he would try to persuade the Hungarian Counterespionage Police to let the Gestapo handle our case. I gave him the address of the Portuguese attaché's home where I knew we would be accepted. Then we parted.

It was time now for Imre to assume his new identity. We filled out Sarika's blank papers, and he became Imre Nagy, an electrician's helper. Since we could not produce a marriage certificate and did not want to live separated, we concocted a story that seemed good enough to us. The wife of Imre Nagy was my sister, but since she was an alcoholic he wanted to divorce her and marry me, an unhappy widow. Meantime I, Maria Kocsmáros, lived with him in sin, pending completion of the divorce. With the papers in our pockets and the story all worked out we left our obstetrician friend and rang the bell of our other friends, the Portuguese attaché and his wife.

We did not arrive at the most opportune moment: they were getting ready for a big party. But I said: "Never mind, I'll stay in the kitchen as your cook, and Imre will be my boyfriend." We forgot only one thing, that there might be some people at the party who might know and recognize us. Early in the evening a lady came into the kitchen to get a glass of water. She looked at Imre. He had been her first love! She was a newspaperwoman, very active in an underground group. She showed no sign of recognition, took the glass of water, and left the kitchen.

Later another lady came into the kitchen together with our hostess. I was kneading dough, and I felt pretty confident that with my bleached hair and bold makeup no one would recognize me. Our hostess thought that this would be a good opportunity to train me for future situations of this type, so she began to talk with the other lady about concert life in Budapest. At one point she said: "I always went to the concerts of Agi Jambor. Lord knows what happened to her." The guest answered: "I did not like her playing at all." My hostess replied: "But she played Bach so beautifully." The answer: "I hate Bach." It was very difficult for me not to throw the dough in her face.

The next morning Mr. Graef visited us, bringing some ration cards with him. He thought that in a few days we could go home. His negotiations with the Hungarian Counterespionage Police were progressing satisfactorily. In a few days he actually did take us home to the yellow-star house. He told the janitor: "I brought these people back, but we are watching them." The people in our apartment received us joyfully. They were all in mourning for us, convinced that we had been killed by the Gestapo. They put us immediately to bed to give us a little rest. We did not have the courage to tell them the truth.

Soon after we got back we noticed that opposite our house there was a man leaning against a tree, watching our window. Mr. Graef told us that he was from the Hungarian Counterespionage Police. We were watched for three weeks, day and night, and when we went out for the permitted hour the counterespionage agent followed every step we took. Our greatest pleasure at this time was to watch the man standing outside on cold and rainy days, fondly hoping that he would catch a cold, or flu, or preferably pneumonia. What our watchdog did not know was that during those weeks our underground group had several meetings in our room, despite him.

There was one more incident that happened in this yellow-star house period that is perhaps worth telling. It was our only encounter with the ordinary police—not the secret police, nor the counterespionage police, nor the Gestapo—just the good old Hungarian police. One morning at the usual time—around 6 o'clock—two policemen came to arrest Imre for stealing eight boxes of instruments from his own laboratory. Imre said to me, "This is fine, I have never been accused yet with such an insignificant crime." You see, to commit sabotage was a capital offense, and to be a Jew was likewise a capital crime, but stealing was a relatively unimportant misdemeanor.

It so happened that Imre really did commit the theft he was accused of. When the Germans occupied Hungary in March, Imre had packed eight boxes full of the most important instruments in his laboratory, got a little truck, and took them to the cellar of the house of his friend and patent attorney. There the boxes were hidden safely until some months later when the Jews were ordered to move into the yellow-star houses. Unfortunately, the house where the boxes were hidden was designated a yellow-star house. At that time Imre was sick in hospital. He realized that the instruments would be lost in a yellow-star house, so he asked me to do something about them.

I had a girlfriend who had an office where she was willing to hide the boxes. I got hold of a truck and moved the boxes to her office. However, I was unable to move them alone, so I asked a man—Imre's most reliable laboratory helper—to help me with the moving. This was a mistake: he later went to the police and informed on us.

So here were the police, come to arrest Imre for stealing his own instruments. Imre said to the two men, "The eight boxes of instruments are my property. Show me a lawbook in which it is considered stealing if a man changes the location of his own property." He happened to have a Hungarian code of laws among his books. He took it off the shelf and handed it to the police officers, saying, "If you can show me in this book that I have committed a crime, you can arrest me."

Anyhow, they took Imre first to their headquarters, then to the office of my girlfriend. She called me up, so I decided to go over too. I took off my yellow star, gave some money to the janitor, and he let me out of the house. In the office I found several of Imre's coworkers—an engineer, a physicist, and two mechanics. They did not return my greetings, but instead made some very nasty statements to the police about Imre and me. In spite of that, in the end things turned out all right. The policemen went through the boxes, they found nothing incriminating, and they let Imre go free.

8

A brief, failed armistice

The autumn was very cold that year. The "Aryans" were allowed to take fuel away from the yellow-star people, thus we had no wood or coal. In our apartment one old lady was dying. We managed to keep her room heated most of the time. Every time there was an air raid, our doctor friend took his satchel down to the cellar empty. He was a huge man, and hiding behind his back Imre or I usually were able to fill his bag with wood or coal.

On October 14, 1944, there were numerous air raids. The haul of fuel was exceptionally good that day, so the next day, which was Sunday, everybody in the apartment could take a bath. There was only one bath allowed per family, but fortunately our family was not large—only two people. It was a gala Sunday for other reasons too. The people of the yellow-star houses were permitted to go out from noon until 4 p.m. that day, an unheard-of exception. It was a gorgeous day. With our doctor friend and his wife, we decided to make an excursion to the mountains of Buda. We took food along and had a picnic outdoors. It was the happiest day in many months.

We started back around 3 o'clock. On the way we heard a radio loudly blaring from an open window: "Horthy has declared an armistice with the Allies." People stopped us on the street and took off our yellow stars. But Imre was not elated over these happy events. He said solemnly, "This is the time to go into hiding. The Arrow Cross will make a putsch, with German backing." Our friends said that Imre had lost his mind. Imre insisted, "Please listen to me. Let us not go home. Come with us to the home of Mr. Pósfay. He has a large apartment, and he will not object if we bring our closest friends with us." (I shall reveal shortly who Mr. Pósfay was.) Our physician friend retorted that Imre was acting absurdly, and he persuaded us to go back to the yellow-star house.

Soon after getting home we sat down for dinner. When we first moved into our apartment, the twenty-five of us jointly bought a bottle of champagne to celebrate the day, sometime in the distant future, when our troubles would be over. So now one of the company suggested we break out the bottle of champagne as this was the day of the armistice, the day when we were able to remove the yellow stars, the hour of our freedom. But Imre cautioned us, "Let's wait a little longer." And our Nazi janitor seconded, "He is right. You will not have enough time to drink it." What he meant—and fondly desired—was that we would all be dead before we finished the bottle.

Suddenly somebody rushed into the apartment and shouted, "Szálasi is in control of the government. We must sew back the yellow stars immediately. Things will be much worse than before." Our physician said, "I know a man in this house who is an anti-Nazi. He is a former patient of mine. He told me once that he has a number of rifles that we can have to defend the house in case of danger." Imre protested, "How can you be so blind? That man is one of the most dangerous Nazis. And how do you propose to defend this house with a handful of rifles, anyhow? We should leave the house at once." The physician's wife said, "Imre, you are all wrong. Szálasi cannot hold the power for more than twenty-four hours." And she taunted Imre with the implication that he was a coward.

Imre was a man who was never afraid of anybody or anything. In those years of mortal danger, I had never seen him frightened in any situation. He was not afraid now—he only thought and saw more clearly than the rest of us. But the result of all this excitement was that he had a very fierce gallbladder attack. The doctor gave him a lot of morphine to put him to sleep. Then the rest of us went down to the janitor's quarters to listen to the radio. Our radio was taken from us long before this. It was clear that the situation in the city was getting worse and worse every minute. I begged our physician to let me awaken Imre and tell him the truth. It was not too late yet to escape from the house. He became very angry with me and bawled me out unmercifully. He said that I would endanger Imre's life by telling him the truth. He shouted that he was the doctor, and only he had the right to make such decisions.

I went back to our room and did not say anything. From time to time Imre half roused himself from the effect of the drug and asked me how things were going. I answered that everything was going fine, but suddenly there was a great commotion in front of the house, and gunfire was heard from the street. Imre crawled out of bed, dragged himself to the window, and looked out. Arrow Crossists were beating and murdering defenseless people out on the streets. My husband looked at me reproachfully. This was the first time since we were married that I lied to him. We both felt that now the end was near—and I felt that I was responsible for it because I had not told Imre the truth.

Gradually, Imre shook off his daze from the morphine, and we decided to escape from the house. Some weeks before I had sent a telegram to our friend, Mr. Erik Magnus in Sweden, asking for his help. He was an influential person in Sweden, and as President of the Orchestra in Göteborg he had known and been friends with us for many years. Within twenty-four hours we received Swedish passports and citizenship papers. We took our Swedish papers and left the house. The janitor did not want to open the door at first, but Imre convinced him that we were citizens of a neutral country, so he let us out.

Only when we were well outside did we begin to think straight and realize what a mess we were in. In the first place, our Swedish papers were no good. According to government regulations all foreigners in Hungary had to appear before the authorities every week for stamping of their papers. Mr. Cserna had taken in our passport several times for stamping, but it became more and more dangerous for him to do it, and in the end he was unable to have it stamped. In the second place, in the excitement, we forgot to take along our false papers when we left the house. Thus we stood there with no identification papers of any kind. It did not help matters that no sooner had we left the house than we ran into two people from Imre's laboratory. They asked us where we were going. We did not answer—we were afraid that they might call the police. We pretended that we did not recognize them and hurried on our way.

We could not go to Mr. Pósfay since the bridges were closed down. We decided to go to my psychoanalyst and ask for refuge there in the meantime. We knew that he, his daughter, and his two-month-old grandchild were hiding in his office—but that was not the whole story. There were some other friends there in addition, so that together with Imre and me there were seven adults and two babies in that small place. The future there looked pretty insecure, especially during air raids, so Imre called Mr. Pósfay and asked him to let us know as soon as the bridges were open. In a few hours his call came: the bridges were open. I was terribly scared to go out on the street, especially since we had no papers, but Imre said jokingly that we must risk something to save our lives. We arrived safely and thus began a new period in our lives—hiding out in the Pósfay apartment.

9

Sweden to the rescue

His Excellency Virgil Pósfay was Hungary's Ambassador to Switzerland back in peacetime, and he held various other distinguished posts in the Foreign Service. Later he became head of the School of Foreign Service in Hungary. He was a diplomat of the old type, a thoroughly fine gentleman in every respect. His son was also in the diplomatic service. In 1941, when Hungary declared war on the United States, young Pósfay was the one who accompanied the American diplomats to the border. He was acquainted with our very dear friends, the Bonbrights, about whom I spoke in the earlier part of my story. When Pósfay left the train, Jimmy Bonbright gave him our name and address and told him: "You must promise me to do everything possible to save the lives of these friends of mine." Young Pósfay promised it, and he looked us up immediately after his return. We became very close friends, and he and his parents came to our home nearly every week.

In 1943 young Pósfay was appointed consul in Istanbul. He took his mother along; he felt that she would be safer in a neutral country. Before he left, he told his father, "I promised the Bonbrights to save the lives of Agi and Imre. Now that I must leave, you will have to take over this responsibility." The old man promised it to his son, and he kept his promise at the risk of his life.

We arrived in the Pósfay apartment without anything except the clothes we had on. There were some other refugees there before us. There was a Jewish woman who had escaped from Újvidék, where there had been a big pogrom; a young Jewish girl with her boyfriend, who had deserted from the Hungarian Army; and a Russian who had arrived somewhat earlier than the Russian Army. Mr. Pósfay's cook knew everything about everybody. Since we had been frequent guests of the Pósfays in the old times, she had no difficulty in recognizing us in spite of Imre's moustache and my blond hair.

Mr. Pósfay moved into a little room and gave us his bedroom with bath. Imre remarked, "We are probably the only people in hiding who have a home with all comforts." The first night we both slept in Mr. Pósfay's pajamas. The next morning Imre said, "I don't think I can survive this war without my American electric shaver." He called Mr. Cserna and asked him to come over to see us. He came, and Imre told him with a serious face, "Mr. Cserna, you must help me out. Please take me back to the yellow-star house. I must get my electric razor." Of course, that was not the only thing we needed. We got into the official police car, and Mr. Cserna drove us back to the yellow-star house. We packed up our belongings, including the most important ones, our false papers. He then drove us around to visit our relatives and friends, first of all my mother and sister. We took food—and a bit of good cheer—to them.

The house where we lived was a three-family apartment house in Buda. Since there was only one common cellar for the entire house, during air raids we always met the members of the other two families. They knew us under our false names. Imre was Mr. Nagy and I was Mrs. Kocsmáros. Mr. Pósfay's cook, Juliska, took this change of personalities very seriously. She decided that Imre and I should do all the work around the house, and she took over the role of an intellectual lady. She took up the study of piano: Imre and I gave her lessons alternately. While she was practicing, Imre and I did the housecleaning, cooking, laundry, and so forth. We even had to eat in the kitchen. Mr. Pósfay, who was accustomed to eating in the dining room in his old-fashioned dinner jacket, now decided to eat with us in the kitchen. Juliska had a boyfriend, a soldier in the Hungarian Army. He always came to the house secretly because Mr. Pósfay had forbidden him to come. When he came, we all had to go into hiding—naturally, as he was not supposed to know that Mr. Pósfay had refugees in his apartment.

One day Imre got in touch with his former assistant, Mrs. Magda Schay. He asked her to kill two of our rabbits and bring them to us, together with some milk from our goats. We hated to live entirely on Mr. Pósfay's hospitality, without con-tributing anything. However, nothing came of this plan. Magda told Imre that the two men from the laboratory whom we had met at the time we were escaping from the yellow-star house had denounced us, and the police had questioned her repeatedly as to our whereabouts. She was quite certain that she was being watched. Thus nothing came of our rabbit and milk feast.

A week later Mr. Cserna took us around again to visit our family and friends. We went back to the yellow-star house. Our physician friend was not there any longer. All men under fifty, including him, had been deported to concentration camps in Germany. His wife was still there. All women under forty had also been deported, but she was over forty. She had a broken leg. A few nights before, the janitor, together with a group of Nazi hood-lums, broke into the apartment and cleaned out all the money, jewelry, and whatever other valuables they were able to locate. In addition, they beat up the people—this was how her leg had been broken. We also found out while making the rounds that at Dr. Tarjan, Imre's friend and coworker, whose name I mentioned before, had committed suicide. He was scheduled to be deported to Germany—and he chose to take a quicker way out.

We did not lose contact during this period with our good friend Mr. Graef either. He did us many kindnesses. One of Mr. Pósfay's former students was active in the underground, and he was caught by the Gestapo. Mr. Graef took messages to him in the jail, and brought messages from him for Mr. Pósfay and others. The old gentleman was so pleased that he offered Mr. Graef the use of his apartment as a hiding place if the Gestapo should detect his activities, so he could escape into hiding. Mr. Graef also brought us ration cards and the latest news from the British radio.

About three blocks from our house there was a small hospital. It was where our son was born and died. This hospital was now under the protection of the International Red Cross. There were one hundred and twenty people there, partly Jews, partly political refugees, partly really sick people. Some of our friends and relatives were there. I had an aunt there with cancer, and a cousin who was married to one of the doctors, who was a yellow-star man. We went to the hospital almost every day. Imre set up in one of the rooms an apparatus for "washing" documents. This meant removing the ink from documents (birth certificates, marriage certificates, etc.) so that one could write false data on them. In Hungary the data were not typed on official blanks as in the United States, but handwritten in ink by authorized persons. The number of false documents in those times must have run into the millions. Perhaps it is no exaggeration to say that very few, if any, of the two or three hundred thousand yellow-star people of Budapest would have survived without these false documents. And the yellow-star people were not the only ones who needed false papers.

One day all the windows of our house were broken by a severe bombing attack. The only place where there were no windows facing the street was our bathroom, so Mr. Pósfay had our beds brought there. From that time on the bathroom became our bedroom. Even meetings of the underground were held in that odd setting.

There were two especially interesting figures in our underground group at that time—a general and a Catholic priest. The general himself was an "Aryan" but his daughters were Jews, since he was married to a lady who, although a devout Catholic, belonged to the Jewish race. He needed some false papers for his daughters, so we asked the priest to steal some blank forms for us from his church. The poor priest could not square this with his conscience, even though he fully realized that the theft would be for a good cause, so he found another solution that worked just as well. He had a friend, an old priest in a neighboring parish, who had no fountain pen. He used ordinary pen and ink to write the birth, marriage, and death certificates of his parishioners, and the ink was easily "washable." Our priest then got the names of various people who were baptised in the church of his old friend, and all we had to do was to ask for copies of their birth and other certificates. The old priest wrote the copies, and we washed them out on Imre's machine.

One day I went with the general to the Swedish Legation to get some protective passports for his daughters. I met there a young man—one of the most handsome young men I have ever seen—in the garb of a Catholic priest. I looked at him, then looked again, and sure enough, I recognized him. Steve was a young conductor whom Imre and I had helped in his musical education. He had practically become a member of our family. Obviously, he was impersonating a priest. I greeted him properly, "Jesus Christ be praised," which is the correct way to salute a priest in Hungary. The correct answer is, "Forever and ever, Amen," but the young rascal answered, "Hello." I said to him very softly, "You donkey, what happened to you?" "I became a Catholic priest, as you see," he answered. Then we withdrew to a corner where he told me his story.

Sometime before, he was being driven on the street, together with a large group of other people, to deportation in a German concentration camp. A Catholic priest saw him, walked up to him, and said, "Come with me." The young man answered, "I can't, they will kill me." However, they soon came to a bend in the road, and he was able to step out of the group. The priest took him to a monastery, gave him a cassock, and provided him with the papers of a deceased priest. Steve then went to one of his former professors and asked for his help. The professor told him that the priest of his church had recently died in a bombing attack, and the community needed a priest. Steve learned very quickly how to baptize, how to bury and perform marriages, and he made a very satisfactory priest. Perhaps I might as well tell the rest of his story here. Steve stayed with his flock for the next three months, until the Germans left. In those confused times nobody realized the deception. His congregation loved him, and they tried to persuade him to stay after the war was over, but he left and became assistant conductor of the opera in Budapest. He is now a professor of music at one of the leading universities in Canada.

The general noticed my long conversation with Steve at the Swedish Legation. He asked me who the young priest was and I told him his story. Just as I finished, a nun entered the legation. The general looked at her, then winked at me, and said, "I guess you will tell me next that that nun is your mother,"

One morning at the usual time, 5:30, the doorbell rang in Mr. Pósfay's apartment. We felt sure that at this hour the visitors would come only from the Gestapo or the Arrow Cross. Our bathroom-bedroom was the nearest to the door, so we were supposed to open it. Imre had in the room about ten papers that he had recently "washed" and dried, and it would have been pretty sad if they had found them on us. In addition, Mr. Pósfay had a gun in his room, which was against the law, and he also had a number of important documents hidden in his bedroom. He had taken these from the Foreign Ministry when the Germans occupied Hungary; he wanted to preserve them from destruction by the Nazis.

Imre immediately began to destroy his papers by flushing them down the toilet as fast as he could. The bell began to ring again, more insistently, so I told Imre I had better go to open the door, otherwise they might break it down and throw in a few hand grenades. When I opened the door three rifles were directed at me, held by three Arrow Crossists. One of them inquired: "Where is Virgil Pósfay?" I answered: "Do you think that I would know where an important man like his Excellency is, or what he is doing?" The leader of the three asked me then who I was. I replied: "I am Mrs. Kocsmáros. I ran away from the Russians with my man, and this goodhearted gentleman accepted us in his house as refugees." The Nazi then inquired: "Is it true that a Russian is hidden in this house?" I answered very emphatically: "No, it is not true."

I wanted to keep the conversation going as long as possible to give Imre and Mr. Pósfay time to hide the incriminating evidence. I talked loud and used as vulgar language as I could imagine—I think I played my role of a former prostitute most satisfactorily. I told them how the Russian soldiers had raped us women, and I bawled them out unmercifully for using their guns against us peaceful citizens instead of fighting the Russians. I even threatened them that I would go back to the Russians. They doubtless felt that this would be a calamitous blow to the Nazi cause, for they listened to me with open mouths, unable to put in a word edgewise.

Finally, Mr. Pósfay appeared on the scene to rescue the Arrow Crossists. In his usual kindly tone he asked: "What do you wish, gentlemen?" The leader of the group said: "My name is Brother Megadja." The Arrow Crossists called each other "brother," just as the Communists call each other "comrade." (Incidentally, Brother Megadja was one of the first Nazis hanged after the war for mass murder.)

I interrupted: "Can I go back to my man now?" Brother Megadja slapped me on the back and said: "Go on back, lass." I departed, and the three Nazis followed Mr. Pósfay into the apartment. They searched the rooms pretty thoroughly, but of course they found nothing. Disappointed, they ordered Mr. Pósfay to go along with them for a hearing. The old diplomat answered: "My good friends, I cannot go with you. I must have my shave and bath first. I shall appear at your headquarters at 8 o'clock sharp." It must have been the first time that the "brothers" had met anyone so calm and collected, so they answered: "All right, we will expect you at 8 o'clock."

After they left, Mr. Pósfay called all of us into his living room. We held a little conference there and decided that in case he did not come back from the hearing in about two hours, we would all disappear from the house. However, to our joy, he came back in less than an hour, telling us that his visit at the Nazi headquarters turned out to be a complete flop. When he got there, he found the three "brothers," together with three girls, in the midst of a drunken orgy, and nobody seemed to be in the least interested in him. Unfortunately, it was not at all certain that the whole story would end there, so he advised us to scatter for two or three days, and he promised that he would keep us posted about what was happening.

Imre and I decided that we would become Swedish citizens again for a while, and went to a "Swedish" house where a considerable part of our family lived. At that time there were two ghettos in Budapest. Most of the Jews and yellow-star people of Budapest were crowded into a ghetto in the center of Pest; this place was surrounded by walls and closely guarded. The other was the international ghetto, where those victims of the Nazis lived who were protected to some extent by one of the foreign legations. This ghetto had no walls, but each house was guarded by its janitor armed with a gun, and no one could enter or leave without permission.

The Swedish house into which we moved had previously been a peaceful apartment house where, among others, some of the pure "Aryan" part of our family had lived. When the house was designated a Swedish house, that is, a house for yellow-star people who were under Swedish protection, they decided to stay on (Aryans who wanted to stay in their own homes did not have to move out). Later, some of the non-Aryan part of our family obtained Swedish protection, and they also moved into this house. When Imre and I moved in temporarily, we shared a room with about eight people. The two of us slept in the same bed with the brother and sister-in-law of Peter Lorre, the American movie star. In this two-room apartment on the fifth floor of the house some twenty people tried to live. It was not an easy life. About the only food we had were peas and beans, supplied by the Swedish Legation.

Imre's brother and his wife lived in the same house on the second floor He was a wonderful mathematician and violinist and, like Imre, he had a very fine spirit. They had with them his ninety-year-old paralyzed mother-in-law and his blind sister-in-law. He visited them every day. All the candles were gone now, so we sat in the evenings in complete darkness. By sitting I mean that my brother-in-law had on one knee his wife and me on the other, and Imre sat somewhere on the arm of the chair. Still, it was not an entirely joyless life, for Imre and his brother held the most inspiring conversations that I have ever heard in my life during these black evenings of "involuntary laziness."

On the third day that we were in the house, December 24, 1944, Imre said that we ought to find out what Mr. Pósfay was doing. It was Christmastime, and we felt that we should remember him for his inexhaustible kindness with some sort of a gift. We had absolutely nothing, but my brother-in-law gave us two books to give him as a present. I decided to take it to him immediately. I took on the identity of Mrs. Kocsmáros and started on the journey. When I reached the streetcar station they told me that there were no more cars going across the bridge to Buda. I was determined to perform my errand anyhow, so I walked.

In the house next to Mr. Pósfay's there was a baker, and I stopped at his store to buy some bread. When I opened my purse to pay him I realized that I had forgotten to bring my identification papers along. This meant great danger because the Arrow Cross was holding constant raids all over the city. People were being examined on almost every street corner. What worried me even more was that Imre would find out that I had left without my papers and would become terribly upset.

I arrived breathlessly at Mr. Pósfay's door and told him: "I do not know what to do, I forgot to bring my papers." Fortunately, Juliska, the cook, immediately came to my rescue and said: "Don't mind it, Mariska, you can go home with my papers and bring them back tomorrow." There was nothing to do but to accept, so I quickly found out from Juliska her entire family history, changed myself from a laundress to a cook, and started back. I arrived home safely. As I expected, Imre had discovered my papers and was worried to death.

The next day was Christmas. The Aryan part of our family succeeded in getting some poppy seeds and sugar, and made the favorite Hungarian dish, noodles with poppy seeds. We sat around in a family circle, almost like in old times, when suddenly a terrific explosion jerked us to our feet. The siege of Budapest had begun.

10

Budapest under siege

On Christmas morning Imre said, "Let's go back to Buda to Mr. Pósfay. We cannot let the old gentleman down." We started out and got as far as the pontoon bridge over the Danube. Here soldiers stopped us, and they did not permit us to cross. They told us Buda was already in Russian hands. There was such a terrific bombing going on that we had to return to the Swedish house.

Our life there continued to be much the same as before. My sister conducted a kindergarten in the house for children who had lost their parents or whose parents were unable to take care of them. Imre taught the older children, mainly to distract their attention from their fears.

My sister's husband was employed by the Swedish Legation. On December 29, when he got back from work in the evening, he told Imre and me that the inhabitants of the three neighboring International Houses had been massacred by the Nazis. They were taken to the shore of the Danube and shot so that their bodies fell into the river. This saved the murderers from the work of burying their victims. He advised us to leave the Swedish house and attempt to save ourselves some other way. We immediately went downstairs to see Imre's brother. We told him the story and tried to persuade him to make preparations for their own escape. He smiled with naive confidence and told us that he had prepared everything long before. He took us to a small hidden window that looked down a dumbwaiter shaft and said that he had been storing there a little food over the past months just for such an eventuality. He added that there was room enough there for ten people.

The next day Imre and I left the house to rent a room as Mr. Nagy and Mrs. Kocsmáros. Two blocks from the Swedish house we found an apartment where they were willing to rent us a room. I say *willing*, because nobody wanted to give us a room since we were supposedly unmarried. We were in the room only about five minutes when Imre went to the window and looked out. He asked me to come to the window and pointed to the street. Across the street, Arrow Cross gangsters were herding yellow-star people out of a Swedish house, beating some of them with the butts of their guns, and leading them toward the Danube for destruction. Imre looked at me and asked: "Could we ever look into each other's eyes if this happens to our family and friends, while we are in comparative safety?" I replied that I could not live with such a thought. So we silently took our hats and coats and returned to the Swedish house.

That night we slept in the apartment of my cousin who belonged to the "Aryan" part of our family. In that apartment were also my mother, sister, her husband, and my nephew who were all of "mixed blood." For all of us there were two beds and three chairs. Some slept on the beds, others on the chairs. We could never undress for sleeping because we never knew at what hour of the night our persecutors might appear and drive us out into the frozen streets. In the same house lived one of the great actors of Hungary, Oszkár Dénes, a comedian and dancer of extraordinary talent. His wife, Rózsi Bársony, also one of the leading stars of musical comedy, did not live there; she was hiding in a Red Cross hospital, working there as a nurse with false papers. We laughed every time we met each other—Rózsi was a natural blond but had her hair dyed black; I was a natural brunette but had my hair dyed blond. It was even funnier when we accidentally bumped into each other in a beauty parlor soon after the siege was over—we had both come to have our hair dyed back to its natural color.

Oszkár Dénes was a lifesaver for all of us. His inexhaustible good humor never left him for a moment. Every evening he gave a performance for us. One of his numbers was an imitation of Agi Jambor giving a concert. He played on an imaginary piano in just the way I played. His mimicry was so perfect that one could tell not only that I was playing, but even the piece I was playing. Our favorite number was a chanson he himself wrote about the Swedish house. Its refrain was: "You don't have a Swedish passport . . . so what?" Once when he was singing it and reached the line "You get a direct hit . . . so what?" the house got a real choice direct hit: one of the walls collapsed right before us. That ended that evening's entertainment. Everybody rushed back to their rooms.

One afternoon I was standing at the window of our room. My ten-year-old nephew was with me, and I told him, "Come to the window, there is a tremendous formation of Russian planes overhead. They are very high up, and they look like a thousand silver birds." My nephew said, "Aunt Agi, you are foolish to stand at the window." I laughed and answered, "Don't you know what Uncle Oszkár says . . . so what?" Apparently I had spoken the magic words. There was a bang and the window blew in, followed by its frame. The shards of glass did not hurt me because my head was covered by a thick wool scarf, which I always wore as a protection against the cold. However, I must have suffered a slight concussion from the blast because from that time on I lost my perfect pitch. If I hear music on the radio or phonograph or coming from another room, I hear everything half a tone higher for a minute or two before it comes down to the right pitch.

On January 3 we celebrated our wedding anniversary, and our friends in the house gave a little dinner party in our honor. My cousin pulled out a jar of honey that was hidden somewhere, and everybody got one tablespoonful of honey for bread. Another had a can of American salmon that we divided among fifteen persons. A third brought a candle, so we had some light, and Denes again performed. That night we could hardly sleep at all. It was terribly cold and we had no blankets. The gunfire was unusually heavy and loud. It was a strange anniversary. Then at 6 o'clock in the morning the police came. Again it looked as though we had reached the end of our journey.

Imre and I quickly decided to try to escape. We took our false papers and rushed upstairs to the top floor. There was an apartment here Imre thought we could use, the apartment of the superintendent of the house. We knew that owing to the constant bombing he was living now in the cellar. He was an Aryan, and the door of his apartment had the official police sign on it: "pure-blooded Aryans live here." Imre broke the door lock and we hid ourselves; I in a wardrobe and Imre under a bed. Almost every minute Imre or I would ask the question, "Should we do this or should we go downstairs?" After a while we heard the police shouting the names "Dr. Imre Patai and Agi Jambor." Imre crawled out from under the bed, got me out of the wardrobe, and said, "Apparently they have our names. If they don't find us they may kill our relatives. Let's go downstairs."

On the way downstairs in the general turmoil we brushed against Oscar Denes. Imre smiled at him and said, "Now, Ossie, is it still 'so what'?" Oscar smiled back and said, "Don't worry, I am going to add a few stanzas to that song yet, after the siege is over."

In our apartment my sister's husband greeted us with the words: "I have a paper here that permits you and your family to move to the Swedish Legation." Sure enough, he had the paper. It was forged, but the police accepted it. They gave us an escort, and guarded by him our whole family went over to the Swedish Legation. The gunfire was heavy in the streets and the walk was slow. We had with us my seventy-six-year-old aunt who had pneumonia and hunger typhoid just then.

Arriving there, the first news we heard was that the head of the Hungarian Division of the Swedish Legation had just committed suicide, because the Arrow Crossist Hungarian government had declared all Swedish citizenship papers and letters of protection invalid. There was a young woman there with a six-month-old baby. The Nazis dragged them to the Danube and shot at her; she fell into the water but she was only slightly wounded. She was able to swim out with her baby and to come back to the Swedish Legation. The baby was hungry and cried continually, and the young woman had nothing to give her. Then the mother began to sing to her child. She sang beautifully, and she kept on singing until the child fell asleep. It was the most heartrending musical experience of my life.

The Swedish Legation was completely desolate. There was nothing to eat; we had no money. The hours passed, and slowly the afternoon twilight descended on the city. Something had to be done. Since Imre and I were the only ones in the family who had false papers, the other members persuaded us to leave them and to attempt to return to Mr. Pósfay.

Outside the snow was falling and the cold bit into our faces. The streets were empty, except for Arrow Cross gangsters here and there with their guns. We zigzagged from corner to corner, trying to avoid the Nazis. Finally, we ran right into the arms of a young Nazi. He looked about eighteen. I quickly gathered my wits and said to him, "Dear brother, would you be willing to help us? We want to go to Buda and we don't know the way. We are refugees from the Russians. Please guide us there." He looked at me and said, "I cannot go to Buda. It is under gunfire." I responded, "Please tell us at least how to get there." He explained to us the well-known route . . . and forgot to ask for our papers.

As we struggled on in the twilight, it suddenly dawned on us what impossible inroads war had made into our conscious minds. At Liberty Square we saw a dead cat and about two yards from it a dead man. Somehow the death of the dumb animal who had nothing to do with politics or Nazism or war had a stronger effect on us than the death of the man lying next to it.

We reached the Chain Bridge. This was the only bridge that was not yet closed. I asked a soldier whether we could cross the bridge. He answered, "You can try it, but you will never reach the other end. Russian planes are constantly circling overhead, and they machine-gun anyone they see on the bridge." But Imre said to me, "Don't be afraid, Agi. We will crawl in the snow, under the chains." We did just that. It took us an hour to reach the other end, ordinarily a ten-minute walk. There was incessant gunfire over us. Parts of human bodies were scattered all around, here a hat with some hair and a bloody ear, there a leg or a torso. When we arrived at the other side Imre remarked, "The chains are not exactly what one would call an ideal protection. Unfortunately, there are holes in them." I looked back at the chains and shivered. Of course, Imre knew all along that the chains had holes in them, but he did not tell me. I might not have dared to cross the bridge.

On the Buda side, at the head of the bridge, there was a little shack. We rushed into that. We did not see that on the top of the shack a German anti-aircraft gun was mounted. Just as we entered, the firing began. Our eardrums almost burst from the terrific noise. The soldiers warned us, "Go back to Pest. Buda is hell." We did not listen to them. We felt that the siege of Buda would be over in a few days, while Pest might hold out much longer. As it turned out, just the opposite happened.

We skipped from one house to another between the Russian and German lines. At one place we stayed about twenty minutes in the gateway of a burning house. In front of the house they were burying somebody. Imre asked who the dead man was and was told it was a German general who committed suicide. He looked at me happily and said, "If German generals are committing suicide, we shall soon be free."

11

Down to the lowest depths

Around 8 o'clock we arrived at our destination, Mr. Pósfay's house. Hungarian and German cannons were set up around it. The doors of all houses in the vicinity were closed—apparently everybody was living in the cellars. We knocked on the door for a long, long time, until finally Mr. Pósfay himself came to open it. In contrast with his usual hearty welcome, this time he did not seem happy to see us back. He told us that somebody had denounced us, and the whole house knew that Imre was not Mr. Nagy and I was not Mrs. Kocsmáros. We found out later that the man who denounced us was Vilibald Szokol, the portrait painter who lived in the apartment next to Mr. Pósfay's. I see no reason not to give his name. He was a cruel, hypocritical, cold-blooded Nazi.

Imre said to Mr. Pósfay, "Please let us in to stay for the night. Tomorrow we shall look for another hiding place. We cannot stay on the street for the night. We have to take our chance." It turned out that we could not get away on the next day either. There was ceaseless fighting in the streets. We stayed about two weeks with Mr. Pósfay.

We went down into the cellar. Juliska's first words were, "Where are my papers?" The poor girl had been without papers since Christmas day, and she remained without papers. When the police escorted us out of the Swedish house, in the excitement I forgot to look for her papers.

The cellar consisted of two small rooms. Here were living about twenty-five people from the house, including two children, and every night some fifty to one hundred soldiers came in from the battlefield to sleep there. Mr. Pósfay arranged things so that everybody had a small board to sleep on, and there were blankets to cover us. He shared his small slab of wood with me, and Imre got a folding chair. We had only one toilet, which was outside the cellar in a little corridor leading to the garden. Almost all day and night there were skirmishes in and around the garden, so that after the first week the door of this toilet looked like a sieve. We were allowed to use it only during the middle of the night—every night there were a few hours when the guns were silent. Even this period was not entirely safe. Mr. Szokol's cook was shot in the leg while sitting on the toilet.

Practically our only food was soybeans. We made soup out of them, and Imre found a way to roast and make coffee out of them. In the end we liked it better than regular coffee, and we kept on using it even after the war! Sometimes the soldiers came in to tell us that a horse had been killed in the street by stray bullets. Imre and other men went out with knives and stood in line to cut a piece from the dead horse.

Every day Imre went up with Mr. Pósfay to his apartment to help him to carry his wonderful library to a safer place. On one occasion the two men were almost killed by a bomb that took away the ceiling above their heads . . . but they did not stop packing the books.

Our life in the cellar did not lack excitement. One day the news came that every man under sixty would be drafted. There was a man among us who claimed to be a deserter from the Hungarian Army. He claimed that he had a friend who could obtain exemption papers from the Arrow Cross for money. Imre said, "We have escaped so far; it would be pretty funny if I would have to die on the battlefield fighting for the Germans." So we tried to persuade the "deserter" to get the exemption papers for us. Since we had no money I gave him a small diamond ring that my father had given me. I shall tell more about this later.

One morning one of the mothers discovered a louse on the dress of her little child. Panic swept through the cellar, for we knew that lice may spread typhus among us. Everybody examined himself, and we found that each one of us had lice—thousands of them. We had not changed our clothes since December 24, and this was the middle of January.

Another morning Imre noticed a little pool of water in the cellar. He reported to Mr. Pósfay that someone must have upset a bottle of water. This was pretty sad: water was a precious commodity. Every time one went out for water, one risked his life. In a few minutes we saw more water on the floor, and in half an hour we had water up to our ankles. Imre rushed upstairs and saw that the whole street was under water. A water main had been hit by a bomb. Again we felt sure that we were lost. We could not go upstairs, and we could not go out to the street. Slowly the water rose higher and higher. We had to set the children on top of a high table, and Imre and Mr. Pósfay began to carry the food and other supplies up the stairs. Then, suddenly, the water began to recede. A work crew must have fixed the main; however, it went down very slowly, a little at a time, and we had to live for about ten days in this terribly damp place.

Our next big excitement was Juliska. One day she refused to work, saying that she did not feel well. Imre examined her and found that she had very high blood pressure, and her pulse was around 150. He immediately sent her to the Red Cross hospital that was a couple of blocks away (I mentioned this hospital earlier). Imre wrote a letter of introduction for Juliska to the head physician who was a friend of ours.

One day passed, two days passed, three days passed, and Juliska did not return. Imre became very restless and decided to go and find out what had happened to her. I begged him not to go, knowing how dangerous it was to go out on the street, but his conscience bothered him; after all, it was he who had sent her to the hospital. The wife of the superintendent of the house, who loved us very much, offered to go out with Imre. In three hours they returned. They had not been able to reach the hospital. The news they brought back was horrible. They were told that four days ago a number of SS men had entered the hospital, and tortured and exterminated all of its inhabitants. The hospital became the headquarters of the Arrow Cross.

We had no idea what had happened to Juliska. She went to the hospital the day after the massacre, and she had no papers. Maybe she was arrested as a Jewish woman, though she did not have a drop of Jewish blood in her veins. Maybe she denounced all of us who were living under Mr. Pósfay's protection in exchange for her life. For days we lived in fear, for her life and for ours.

Finally, after about a week, Juliska arrived, happy and gay, clean and rested. But she told us a harrowing story. When she rang the bell in the hospital a Nazi opened the door. She gave him Imre's letter. He read it, looked at her, and asked, "Are you Jewish?" She said, "No, I am not." He asked for her papers, and she had to confess that she had no papers. They arrested her and tried to get information out of her about Mr. Pósfay and his household, but she gave no information. She claimed that she had had a very tough time. Poor Juliska—nobody believed her. She did not look as though she had spent a week in a Nazi jail. I still don't know what had really happened, but I do know that in nine months she gave birth to a healthy child.

One day, toward the end of January, a group of the soldiers who had left their fighting positions to sleep in the cellar at night brought in a quantity of flour, sugar, and fat, and like little boys asked me to bake biscuits for them. In return they promised to give me honey and bread. Since I did not know much about baking, Imre helped me, and together we baked all afternoon and evening. We exercised all the willpower we could muster and managed somehow not to take any of the biscuits for ourselves. They were hungry days—but we did not take any. The soldiers too kept their promise, and they gave us bread and honey. Immediately we put aside the largest share of it for Mr. Pósfay. We gave it to the refugee woman from Újvidék I mentioned before. She was now acting as the housekeeper for Mr. Pósfay. The next morning Imre proudly reported to Mr. Pósfay that we had some bread for him, and asked the housekeeper to give it to him. "Bread? You must be crazy. What bread?" she demanded without expression. I was furious. "Give him the bread we baked yesterday," I shouted. Finally, after entreaties and threats, she confessed that she had exchanged the bread with the soldiers for cigarettes.

The woman was angry. She decided to have her revenge. She went to Vilibald Szokol, who had denounced us once before while we were away from the house, and told him that it was high time to get rid of us. She told him that Imre frequently went out, drew circles in the snow, and gave signals to Russian airplanes to help them locate the Hungarian and German batteries. Szokol went to Mr. Pósfay and threatened that unless he chased us out of the house by the next morning, he would report us to the Arrow Cross. That would mean death, not only for Imre and me, but also for Mr. Pósfay, who had so unselfishly hidden us from the Nazis.

Mr. Pósfay told this to me—he did not dare tell it to Imre for fear of causing a heart attack. He realized that chasing us out into the street would probably mean death for us—there was ceaseless gunfire and fighting in the streets. He expressed his complete willingness to keep us in the house and told me that he would not care to survive without us, anyhow.

I told Imre just how things stood, and he immediately decided that we should leave the house. We were entirely in Szokol's hands. He not only knew our true identities, but he also knew that we had tried to buy false papers for Imre to save him from the draft. The man in the cellar, who claimed that he was a deserter from the Hungarian Army, was really an agent provocateur. He had taken my ring, and then told Szokol all about it. Our only choice was whether only Imre and I should die, or all three of us, including Mr. Pósfay, should die. Needless to say, we chose the first alternative.

Before we left, the janitor of the house came to us and offered to hide us in his apartment. It turned out that he had known who we were all along. He was the father-in-law of a man who had worked in Imre's factory, and Imre and he liked each other very much.

Nevertheless, we did not accept the offer. The apartment was aboveground, and to live aboveground at that time and at that place was almost equivalent to a death sentence. The next morning we left the house, carrying a little handbag containing a small piece of bread. For a whole day we struggled in the snow through minefields and burning houses. We begged friends to give us a corner in their cellar, but not a single person would accept us. Some of these men were friends of twenty years. One of these so-called friends, whose wife was the most brutal to us, has now a very high position in Communist Hungary.

Finally, about dark, we arrived at Rózsadomb, at the house of Mr. Harsanyi, Imre's friend and patent attorney. He had been one of the witnesses at our marriage—so long ago it hardly seemed believable. He told us that there were a number of Nazis in his cellar; he would take us in on the following day, but first he would have to prepare the ground. In the meantime, he suggested, we should spend the night in his garage.

The garage was used as a stable for the soldiers' horses. In addition to the horses, there were two soldiers there. We had not eaten all day, but we offered them part of our small piece of bread. This broke the ice, and they told us that they were on the verge of deserting. They cursed Hitler for his war, and for robbing them of their sons. Then we lay down to sleep under the horses. The garage was small and full of horses—the only free space was occupied by the two soldiers.

In the middle of the night we were awakened by a peculiar sensation. We found ourselves soaked by a warm shower. Somehow this seemed to be the final straw. We felt terribly disgusted and despondent. Imre said, "I think we have come to the end of the road," and began looking for the little bottle of potassium cyanide that he always carried with him during the last few months. Fortunately, it turned out that he had forgotten to put the poison in the bag. I did not agree with Imre; I was not yet convinced that everything was lost. Still, I am not sure that I would be here now if Imre had not forgotten the cyanide.

During the night Mr. Harsanyi told his wife and son that Imre and I would join the inhabitants of his cellar the following day. He thought it advisable to introduce us to the others, not as friends, but as strangers who had fled from a burning house. The next morning something happened that made an even better story. The neighboring garage got a direct hit and was completely demolished. The garage where we stayed was quite close to it, so that we were thrown around a little by the blast. Mr. Harsanyi rushed upstairs to find out what had happened to us, and other people also gathered around the scene. They started digging, and in a short time the six people who were in the garage were brought out of the rubble. Mr. Harsanyi asked the bystanders whether there was anyone among them who knew first aid. Imre immediately volunteered. He was able to help three of the people, but the other three were dead. Among the latter was a little girl.

After that, Mr. Harsanyi invited us to stay in his cellar. We stayed there for two weeks. It was not really a cellar, but a basement under the cellar, which had been dug to hide people from the Nazis. There were six people in this subcellar before we came: Mr. Harsanyi's son, Steve, who had deserted from the Hungarian Army, a trapeze artist with his wife, a dancer, a well-known Hungarian actress, and another girl. Our arrival made the number eight. There were only two beds for the eight of us. The place was in complete darkness. Under the subcellar there was yet a third cellar, which was so deep underground that its floor was covered with water. Whenever Nazi raiders came to look for Jews or army deserters, Mr. Harsanyi sent us a signal by tapping on the floor of the top cellar; then we went down to this third cellar. Sometimes we spent hours there kneeling in the water until the Nazis left.

Mr. Harsanyi supplied us with food. We had a pail that was our substitute for a toilet, and we permitted ourselves to use it only once a day. Every night a different person had to carry it upstairs and empty it in the snow. Imre would never let me do it—he did it for both of us. The person who went upstairs had to carry another bucket too. This was to be filled with snow, which was our drinking water.

We never knew what time of day it was, for there was darkness around us all the time. Still, we were not completely unhappy—in fact, I might say almost without exaggeration that we had a pretty good time. Imre and Steve invented a number of quiz games that we played endlessly. The dancer toyed with the idea that after the war he would do interpretive dances to all forty-eight preludes and fugues of Bach. I had to hum for him all the themes, and he would dance in the dark. We did not see him, but he described the steps. He is now manager of one of the leading theaters of Amsterdam.

There were occasional excitements to make life even more interesting. Once we almost beat the actress up because she washed her hands twice in one day, and thus deprived us of some of our drinking water. Another night we heard a lot of noise upstairs. German soldiers entered the house and robbed Mr. Harsanyi of his belongings. They were very drunk; they played the piano and sang loudly, while we sat in the cellar and trembled for our lives.

Thus we spent two weeks in the "slum." This was the fond name we gave to our hiding place, because other cellars were almost luxurious compared to ours. At the end of that time Mr. Harsanyi came downstairs, opened our door, and announced that we were liberated. The Russians had taken over part of the street, and we were free.

Olga Jambor (née Riesz) Agi's mother.

Musical friends in the early 1930s.

Agi, shortly before the war.

Prewar passport. Courtesy of David Percy.

View of Pest
and the bombed
Chain Bridge.

View of Buda and the bombed Chain Bridge.

Agi's godson who died in Auschwitz.

Agi and Imre in America.

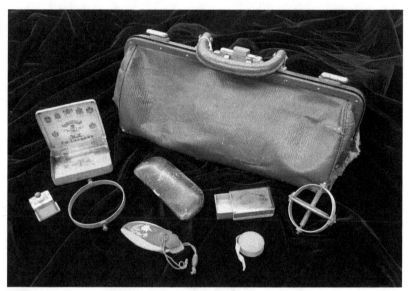

All of Agi and Imre's possessions carried in this bag in 1945.
Courtesy of David Percy.

Agi restored to health after the war.

Imre Patai, Agi's husband.

Agi in 1950.   Agi in the mid-1950s.

United States of America
State of .... Pennsylvania .... }
County of .... Philadelphia .... } s.s.

In the matter of application of Agi Jambor (Agnes Jambor Patai)
for passport facilities:

I Agi Jambor (Agnes Jambor Patai) whose occupation or profession is that of
___Concert Pianist_____ residing at 1414 Spruce Street, Philadelphia 2, Penna.
1414 Spruce Street
[Number]   (Street)   Philadelphia 2   Penna.
                              (City or Town)   (State, District, Territory)
being duly sworn, depose and say:

1. I was born at Budapest, Hungary____ on the 4th day of February 1909
    I have lost my nationality of origin owing to because I have refused
    to return to communist controlled Hungary

2. I am unable to obtain a passport or any form of travel document from the
    Government of the country in which I now reside.

3. I attach hereto my photograph and personal description as evidence of
    identity.

4. I am urgently desirous of traveling to___ Sweden _____for
    following reason:__ recuperation of health and concert tour

A stateless Agi attempting to visit Sweden from the United States in 1948.
Courtesy of David Percy.

EIGHTIETH SEASON
1949 — 1950

PHILADELPHIA MUSICAL ACADEMY

1617 SPRUCE STREET, PHILADELPHIA

JANI SZANTO, President-Director

Announcing . . .

TWO SERIES OF LECTURE RECITALS

by AGI JAMBOR Distinguished Pianist

Press Comments—

"AN ARTIST OF RARE DISTINCTION"
Edwin H. Schloss, Phila. Inquirer

"PHILADELPHIA HAS BEEN FORTUNATE
TO WELCOME THIS EXCEPTIONAL MUSI-
CAL PERSONALITY TO ITS MIDST"
Max de Schauensee, Evening Bulletin

"A GIFTED ARTIST WITH POWER AS
WELL AS POETRY IN HER WORK"
Noel Strauss, New York Times

"STRENGTH OF TEMPERAMENT AND
MUSICALITY—GRACE AND POETIC FEEL-
ING"
A. Eversman, Washington (D.C.) Star

EIGHTEEN LECTURES AND PROGRAMS

*"Psychological and Spiritual Analysis of
Musical Interpretation"*

FORTNIGHTLY ON FRIDAYS AT EIGHT P.M. - STARTING SEPTEMBER 23rd, 1949

EIGHTEEN LECTURES AND PROGRAMS

"Beethoven's Thirty-Two Piano Sonatas"

FORTNIGHTLY ON FRIDAYS AT EIGHT P. M. - STARTING SEPTEMBER 30th, 1949

An early concert in America. Courtesy of David Percy.

Meeting President Truman in 1948. Courtesy of Associated Press.

Claude Rains, Agi's second husband, in 1959.

Agi in the late 1950s.   Agi in her early eighties.

Buda on the left and Pest on the right. Courtesy of David Percy.

12

Freed in Buda, desperate trek to Pest

We climbed up into the light. The first thing we discovered was that we were blind. The last two weeks had been spent in complete darkness. When our eyes became accustomed to the light we saw two Russian soldiers there in white ski suits, with long beards. It was like something out of a Dostoevsky novel. We cried and embraced them. They could not speak any language other than Russian, but it did not matter. They gave us warm soup and bread, and that spoke more eloquently than any language.

Our joy was boundless. But good things seldom last long. Soon a neighbor came in and told us that the two men were not really Russian soldiers, but German agent provocateurs, and that we had fallen into a trap. This turned out to be a lie, but it gave us a bad fright. Hardly had we recovered from this when another scare came—a more serious one. A Russian captain came into the house. He could speak German, so we were able to talk with each other. He warned us that we would have a very tough time with the Russian soldiers since they—the officers—were unable to control them. He said that he was terribly ashamed of their behavior, but he could not take the responsibility for what might happen to any or all of us.

This captain was a strange, sad, broken man. He had been a high school teacher of Latin before the war. He wanted to adopt the little granddaughter of Mr. Harsanyi and take her to Russia.

His entire family had been killed by the Germans, and he was afraid to go back home, alone, where no one would be waiting for him. He took out his bank book and showed Mr. Harsanyi the amount of money he had saved, and offered it all in exchange for the girl. When Mr. Harsanyi refused the offer with kind and sympathetic words, the captain wept like a child.

We had plenty of trouble the next few days. Drunken soldiers were continually coming and going and kept bothering us. In addition, we were constantly under gunfire by the Germans. Because of this the captain advised us to go to another part of Buda, which had been taken earlier, around Christmas, and the Germans were nowhere near that area. He said that we had suffered enough—it was silly to suffer any longer. He gave us a paper vouchsafing that we were reliable people who did not collaborate with the Germans. But he warned us that the trip would not be easy. Some of the streets were still full of mines covered with snow, and street fights were still going on here and there with German snipers.

Three days after our liberation the eight of us, graduates of the "slum," decided to face the new adventure. Progress in the snow was very difficult—our eyes were still weak, and the snow blinded us. We went through deserted minefields, rubble and ruins, and burning houses, but we felt happy and gay. We sang and laughed; the existence of being hunted animals was over. We were free; we were human beings again. It was a motley crew. Our clothing was fantastic. I wore Mr. Harsanyi's slacks and even his underwear. To celebrate the liberation I had indulged in the luxury of washing my undies in the snow—after eight weeks of continuous wear. But in the damp, cold house they did not dry, so I had to borrow a pair of drawers from Mr. Harsanyi. He was a stout man; I had to wear them wrapped around me and pinned over with a safety pin. I wore them until we got to Sweden in 1946; I had nothing else.

The Russian soldiers we met on the way allowed us to pass when they read the captain's paper. Only once did we get stuck, and it seemed that we would not be allowed to continue our journey.

But then Imre took from his pocket a tube of sulfa drug, gave it to the soldier, and we were allowed to continue. This walk in normal times would have taken about an hour, but this time it took a day. We arrived at the district of Hűvösvölgy around 6 o'clock in the evening and reported at the police station for a room for the night. They asked for our identification papers, and all we had were our false Nazi papers. We tried to explain to them who we were, but they laughed and said that anybody could say that. It looked for a while as though the new Hungarian police would put us into one of the old jails of liberated Budapest, but we got a lucky break. One of the police officers, who was formerly an actor, recognized the actress in our group. He also knew Imre and me by name, and he was willing to go to his chief and swear as to our identity.

After that we were treated very nicely. They advised us to burn our false papers as fast as we could, which we did. Imre had no shirt, so they gave him a lady's blouse, and he wore it for a long time. He had nothing better to wear. They gave us one towel and one pot to cook in—to be sure it was not quite adequate for eight people, but that was all they had. They assigned us an apartment in a three-apartment building, where according to the police chief we would be completely safe. There was a high Russian Army officer, a colonel, living in one of the other apartments—a former university professor of mathematics. He was the commander of the troops in the vicinity, and he did not permit any soldier to enter the house.

We arrived in our beautiful little apartment around 8 o'clock. There was absolutely nothing in it except some straw on the floor that the German soldiers had left there—and millions of lice. Let me tell you a curious thing about lice. All my life I had been plagued with allergies of all sorts. There was hardly anything I ate, smelled, or breathed in that did not give me a rash. Now, after having been infested with lice for three months, I lost all of my allergies, and to this day they have never returned. Imre said jokingly that after the war that he would raise lice and make an extract to be used as a serum against all allergies.

Imre used the straw for making a fire, and this was the first time that we were in a warm room that winter. The next morning Imre made a deal with the janitor. He undertook all the necessary repair work around the house, in exchange for which the janitor promised to give us some food. The deal completed, Imre returned, triumphantly carrying a big tray with hot tea, bread, and some old fat that we spread on the bread. He brought some good news, too. There was an apartment above us, completely furnished—and empty. Its owner, a Nazi woman, had fled to the West with her friend, an SS officer. Imre quickly made an inventory of her belongings, and then we brought down to our apartment her chairs and beds. There were two and a half beds now for the eight of us—half a bed more than we had in the "slum." The actress and I had a wonderful time rummaging about in the upstairs apartment. We read all the love letters the SS officer wrote to the lady, and then we found some eau de toilette and rouge, which we tried out immediately on our dirty faces.

A few days later a Russian soldier came into our room and said, "*Davaj robotni*" ("Go to work"). Imre was away at that time. The actress said no—she did not want to spoil her hands. The others also refused to work. But I felt that it was better to work and have a little food than to starve. So I said, "I'll work." They brought me a huge basket of dirty clothes and gave me two large cakes of soap, and I became a laundress again. This time I did it under my own name and not as Maria Kocsmáros.

There were two occasions when I stole during the war. The first time I stole wood—I told about this before. The second time I stole water. The soldiers brought me a large tub of hot water for the laundry. Before I started washing the clothes we all took baths in the washtub—our first bath in months. Then we washed our own underwear, and then came the clothes of the Russians.

One day, while I was doing the washing, a Russian officer wandered into the laundry room. He looked at me for a while silently, then he asked me in German, "Do you speak German?" I said, "Yes." "You were not always a washerwoman," he stated. "How do you know?" I inquired. "Because you are doing a pretty bad job as a laundress," he responded. My feelings were hurt. "Look," I said, "I did not ask you what you did before the war." "Why not?" he answered with dignity. "I am not ashamed to tell you. I was the first clarinetist in the Leningrad Symphony Orchestra."

I told him then that I was a concert pianist. Then he was terribly ashamed that I had to do this kind of work. He inquired about Imre and the others, and I related to him our story. A few hours later several trays of food arrived in our room with meat, potatoes, and wine—enough for eight people. In the evening the officer came to our room and said that he had brought a piano. He asked if I would like to play for a small group. He invited Imre and the six others too, and we improvised a little concert. I remember the first piece I played—after six months of idleness—it was "Chaconne" by Bach, in Busoni's transcription. I played them some jazz and some waltzes too, in the hope of improving our food supply. There was a Don Cossack officer in the group; he sang, and I accompanied him.

After that I had to play every evening. During the day I washed or ironed; in the evenings I played for audiences of fifty to one hundred people, mostly Russian officers and soldiers. Imre did various repair jobs and tried in many little ways to improve our living conditions. One thing I remember is that he found a way to make a candle burn much longer. In the meantime both of us kept begging the professor-colonel in our house to help us to go to Pest to visit our family. He declined repeatedly; he felt that after having survived thus far, it would be foolish to lose our lives in an attempt to go through the battle lines. He promised every day that the siege of Buda would be over the next day—but the days passed and the siege continued.

Imre made several attempts to get a job through the police. He was starved for work. He was willing to take any kind—technical, teaching, clerical, anything—but all his efforts failed.

Once, while at the police station, he met one of the engineers from his former factory. This man had denounced him to the Germans as a saboteur, so it was not his fault that we were still alive. He was there with his wife and two children, and of course he was scared to death when he saw Imre. But Imre went to him, shook hands, and started a friendly conversation with him. The engineer told him that he had to leave his house because it was under constant fire, and now he sat on the street with his family. Imre immediately went to the actor-police officer and begged him to assign a home to the family of our would-be murderer; then Imre went and got food for the engineer's hungry children. I tell this because that man remained one of our bitterest enemies and tried in every way possible to harm us in the new Hungary too.

On another occasion, when Imre visited the police headquarters, he met the former president of the Psychoanalytical Society. He was also homeless, together with his sister and his very old mother. At that time there were nine of us living in our apartment. "Why not twelve?" said Imre with a smile and a shrug of his shoulders, and he brought home the three additional members of the household. (I should have mentioned before who the ninth member was. A Russian soldier had asked our permission to join us a while before. He was a kindly, funny, lonely little man. His name was Fischer, and he had a job of extreme importance—he was a cook.)

The first day I saw that the psychoanalyst scratched himself very frequently. I told him to go to the bathroom and get rid of some of his lice. He blushed with indignation, and he stated proudly that he was the head of a hospital in Budapest—he had no lice. I touched my own dress, and showing him what I had in the palm of my hand I said, "Look, I am quite certain that you have as many as I. I am a concert pianist myself, but these lice don't know it." Imre went to the bathroom with him and helped him to get rid of at least a hundred lice.

One night around 2 a.m. I was awakened by a woman who came to get from me the laundry of the Russian soldiers, drying in the attic. There was a terrific din on the street. Mr. Fischer, the cook, ran in breathless and explained to us what had happened. About ten thousand German soldiers who were defending the Royal Palace were making an attempt to break through the Russian lines and to get away. Apparently the attempt was at least partly successful because the Russians were evacuating our neighborhood.

Here was this desperate worry again, that we would fall into German hands once more. Imre asked the colonel to take us along, and he very kindly took us in his car. However, he was not alone, and the other officer in the car may have outranked him—anyhow, we were told that civilians were not allowed in officers' cars; we would have to go with the soldiers. The colonel helped us to get on a truck jammed full of soldiers, but as soon as he drove away they tossed us off the truck into the snow. Several more trucks came, until finally one of them accepted us.

Imre was sitting next to a very young soldier. The boy was trembling. He could not have been more than seventeen. Imre put his arms around him and said to him in Hungarian, "Little fool, don't be afraid." Then he pulled out his stopwatch and began to count the time elapsing between the flashes and the roar of the guns. We were getting closer and closer to the firing line. Finally, we were so close that Imre said to the Russian—in Hungarian—"Now you are completely justified to tremble."

The truck turned around, and we began to believe that we were getting away from the Germans. However, in a few minutes it stopped, and we were thrown out on the street again. It was the middle of the night, and we were surrounded by snow and darkness. We began to walk back to our house. Guards on the street asked us for the password, which we did not know. We could have gotten into trouble, but then I suddenly remembered the word, "*artistka*," which meant that I was an artist. Some of the soldiers may have attended my concerts and recognized me—at any rate it worked, and we were allowed to pass.

We managed to get back to our house. Here the atmosphere was completely changed; we had no friends any longer. They expected that the Germans would be back in a short while. A fierce battle raged on the streets.

For two days and two nights our house was in "no-man's-land." Then, suddenly, our dear cook, Mr. Fischer, appeared on the scene. He had white gloves on his hands and at least one ring on each of his ten fingers. He carried two swords on his belt, and he told us that he had killed at least two hundred Germans. It did not in the least diminish our joy that his story was slightly exaggerated. Soon the colonel came, and when we asked him about the heroic exploits of Mr. Fischer, he told us that although Mr. Fischer could make the most excellent steaks, he did not know the butt of a gun from the handle. He had, it seemed, stolen his loot from the Royal Palace—they were things the Germans left there.

The colonel also told us that we should cross the Danube and go over to Pest as soon as we could. "Buda is finally liberated," he said, "but now thousands of Russian soldiers will arrive from the battlefields, and it would be best to clear out before they came." He was very busy, he could not stay at home to protect us, and he would be very sorry if we had bad experiences with the soldiers. Pest was already somewhat better organized, since the liberation had taken place a few weeks earlier. We listened to him and decided to follow his advice.

The eight of us, the alumni of the "slum," set out for Pest. The road on the Buda side was about two miles long, and the entire road was covered with dead soldiers, mostly Germans. We had to climb over hills of dead bodies. Some of the corpses were flattened out like pancakes from the tanks that had passed over them. The old gray slacks I wore were bloody up to my knees. I was so constituted that I felt like fainting when I saw even a chicken killed. Now the sight of all these dead people somehow made no impression on me—I was unable to feel a thing. But still, I saw one thing that I cannot forget. As we passed a cellar, with its door blown wide open by a direct hit, I saw a mother sitting there inside with her child in her arms—both dead—still simply sitting there.

Finally we reached the Danube. Although it was frozen over, the ice was not completely firm. The six others decided to cross over the ice anyhow, but I didn't dare, and Imre stayed with me. We looked for canoes without success. I felt the beginnings of hunger typhoid coming over me, so we decided to go to Mr. Pósfay's house, which was not far from there.

One of the symptoms of hunger typhoid—the worst one—is diarrhea. I looked desperately for a toilet but could not find any. I asked people. One man pointed upward and replied that there was one hanging on the outside of a window five floors up. That left me only one alternative . . .

We finally reached Mr. Pósfay's house and knocked on the door, and who opened it but our dear friend, Mr. Szokol. Instead of apologizing to us, instead of begging our forgiveness, he said: "Oh, I am so happy to see you. I was so worried that something might happen to the two of you." Then Mr. Pósfay came. Taking one look at me, he gave me opium—the only drug available at that time in Budapest for hunger typhoid. Then Juliska came in a beautiful silk velvet dress, with diamond rings and earrings. She had quickly exchanged her Nazi friend for a Russian friend.

We stayed in Mr. Pósfay's house. At the end of the week I felt strong enough to attempt the crossing to Pest again. Mr. Pósfay gave us 800 pengős to add to the 200 we had. The money did not last long. When we reached the Danube again there were thousands of people waiting for canoes. Imre shouted: "I will give a thousand pengős to anyone who takes us across." Magically, a canoe appeared, and we were on our way. Just when we reached the middle of the Danube, a mine exploded near us. It did not hurt anybody, but it did not help the water phobia that I have had all of my life.

We arrived safely in Pest. We walked miles to reach our own apartment. It no longer existed. Then we went to the yellow-star house apartment. It was burned out. Then we went to the Swedish house. Here we found Imre's brother, who told us that my aunt had starved to death, but the rest of the family was alive. They had gone back to my sister's original apartment.

Our peregrination ended in my sister's apartment. My mother, sister, brother-in-law, and nephew were all there. They did not recognize us until we began to speak. Then all of us cried from joy. They thought we were dead. Some people even told them that they had seen our corpses. We did not dare to let them embrace us—we were so infested with lice.

We got rid of the lice by hanging our clothes out the window. It was subfreezing weather, and the lice fell off the clothes dead. We went to bed and slept for twenty-four hours; we were terribly weak and tired and sick. My sister made pancakes for us from dried peas, which she ground into a flour. They were delicious.

So ended World War II for Imre Patai and Agi Jambor. And so began the peace—a peace almost worse than the war.

13

A peace worse than the war

Two days later Imre and I started to look for jobs. We no longer had a single cent. Imre's factory was still occupied by the people who were put there by the Nazis, and who persecuted us. He was not admitted into his own factory. He tried to get a job in another radio factory but was refused there, too. I tried to get a job at the Academy of Music. They did offer me a job, to teach piano to the students of wind instruments. All students at the academy had to learn at least the fundamentals of piano. I might have accepted it, but the salary was practically nil, and we needed money badly. We were living on my sister, and she was in a pretty labile financial situation, too.

As compensation for our suffering under the Nazis, we were permitted to eat once a day in the people's free kitchen. Imre got his lunch at the engineers' kitchen, and I got mine at the musicians' kitchen. It consisted of bean soup filled with dirt and trash—they had no time to wash the beans before cooking, nor to wash the pots. The rest of the time we ate at my sister's.

I tried to get a job at the Orchestra Society as a soloist. They did not want me. Pest had been liberated earlier than Buda, and the musicians of Pest filled all the available jobs. They were not interested in helping the latecomers. Week after week Imre and I walked the streets of Pest, trying to get jobs. In the evening we returned home, dead tired from failure and humiliation, the only result of the day—a cup of free bean soup.

Imre decided to sue for the return of his factory, but the case against the Nazis sitting in the factory progressed very slowly. On their side was money and power, and on our side was only right. Money counted more.

Finally, we began to get some work. Imre acquired some little odd jobs here and there. I got a few pupils. We found an apartment. It had no windows, of course, and we had to share it with two young girls because we could not afford to rent one alone. The girls' father was a Jewish physician, and both parents had been killed by the Nazis. The four of us lived in one room. This room had been used by German soldiers as a toilet, since the toilet on the floor had been stolen by somebody. I went to the owner of the house who was a good amateur pianist and said that I would teach him to play all of Beethoven's sonatas in exchange for a toilet. His answer was: "My dear child, today a toilet is worth more than Beethoven's sonatas." So we had to struggle along without a toilet.

We got back Imre's library—or what was left of it. It had been used as a barricade when the Germans defended the house against the Russians during the siege. We got back my two pianos—we found them in two different houses. But life still continued to be unbearably difficult. During the years of persecution we were kept alive by the dream that after the war Imre would return to his laboratory and I to the concert stage. Now our dreams collapsed. We were desperately disappointed.

જી

One day, Mr. Zathureczky, a violinist, and at that time president of the Academy of Music, told me that he was to give an after-dinner concert in the house of someone from the American Legation. He asked me whether I would be willing to accompany him in exchange for a free dinner. I refused because Imre was not invited. But when the evening came a big car from the American

Legation arrived in front of our house, and the chauffeur came in and announced that he was to take me to the dinner. It was impossible to say no, so I followed him to the car.

On the way to the home of our host I talked with the chauffeur. He was an American of Hungarian descent and spoke some Hungarian. He told me that he was a factory worker in America, and that he earned enough money to own a car and a radio, and he had a bathroom with hot water, and he went to the movies once or twice a week—things that had become to us only dreams of the past. I listened to him spellbound and could not believe that such a way of life still existed anywhere in the world.

When I entered the house I saw electric lights for the first time in a year. The crowd was very elegant, and I felt pretty much out of place—I had no stockings and wore a pair of heavy, old climbing shoes, and a very old black dress.

The guests were headed by Mrs. Schoenfeld, the wife of the American minister. Her daughter was also there, who was a pianist. Many people from the American Military Mission were there. And I met after a long time our very dear and loyal friend, Count Szapáry, who had been a member of the board of directors of Imre's factory.

It was the first time in ages that I saw a dinner table set with a tablecloth, napkins, glasses, and silver. When I saw the food on the table I felt that I could not eat a bite of it, for I was afraid that I would burst into hysterical tears. I remembered Imre at home with his bowl of weak soup. I pretended to have an upset stomach and did not eat anything, not even the ice cream, which looked heavenly. After dinner we played with Mr. Zathureczky, and then I played alone. Our host was the agricultural attaché of the American Legation, Mr. Harry Le Bovit.

A few days later a little sunshine came into our lives. A letter came from Sweden, from Mr. Eric Magnus, whose name I have mentioned before. When we were most disillusioned and depressed, we had frequently thought of leaving Hungary. We thought of America, but we knew it was only a mirage, which could never become reality. When this letter arrived, we immediately thought that we might immigrate to Sweden.

At that time there was no mail service between Hungary and other countries, so we were at a loss as to how to communicate with Mr. Magnus. Then the thought occurred to me that Mr. Le Bovit might help us. I went to the American Legation and asked to see him. He was very kind and sent my letter to Sweden via the American Legation at Oslo. At the same time he asked me whether I would be willing to give piano lessons to his wife. I accepted gratefully, and after that for a while we lived almost entirely on the money I earned from the Le Bovits.

I gave the first lesson on a Saturday. Both Imre and I were invited to spend that weekend with the Le Bovits. From a materialistic point of view that weekend was one of the great events of our lives. We took hot baths twice a day. We were served by a maid three hot meals a day. After dinner we had chocolate. Those Hershey bars were the finest chocolate we had ever had. Imre and I thought we would never see such wealth again.

Imre played chamber music with Mr. Le Bovit, who was a good violinist. We told the Le Bovits our story, and Harry said: "Dictate to me your story, and I will write a book about it. Your name will be known before you arrive in the United States." But nothing came of that book.

We looked at the Sunday edition of the *New York Times*. I saw the concerts advertised in New York and was astounded at the wealth of famous concert artists America had acquired. I remarked to Harry: "My name will never appear on this page. You have so many great pianists." And I asked him: "Do you think that once I might play in the Times Hall in New York?" I knew from the papers that Times Hall was the smallest concert auditorium in New York. He answered: "In America we say that nothing is impossible." Little did I know that four years later I would play to a sold-out house in Carnegie Hall.

We were invited to the Le Bovits' home after that for every weekend, and these weekends became the highlights of our existence. Harry gave me the first concert dress I owned after the war. They made us take vitamins, and they gave us orange juice, condensed milk, chocolate, and so forth. At the same time we began to receive packages from the Bonbrights, who were back in the United States. They found out from the Red Cross where we were living and sent us a big package regularly every month. I wonder whether the Americans realized what these packages meant to us. It was not only that these packages contributed in a great measure toward saving our lives, but they did much more than that: they saved our self-respect. After all the frustrations and humiliations, after the loss of old childhood friends, to know that we still had some friends who cared for us, who loved us—it is impossible to describe what this meant in our lives.

The Le Bovits soon arranged a concert for me in their house. Practically all Americans in Budapest were invited. The result of this was that I began to get more and more American pupils, partly from the Military Mission, partly from the Legation.

Eventually we received an answer to our letter from Mr. Magnus. He wrote that our visas for Sweden were ready. We immediately began to go after the passport and the Russian exit permit. Imre began to develop plans for his research work in Sweden and also started to study English very intensively. In addition, he spent a good deal of time on the fight to get back his factory, but things progressed very slowly—the papers, the lawsuit, everything.

Christmas 1945 came, and the Le Bovits gave us a big turkey and a chocolate cake as presents. On Christmas Eve we were their guests, and that was the time when I was first introduced to American music. Somebody played "Yankee Doodle," and I sat down and wrote symphonic variations of it for piano and violin. I gave it to Harry Le Bovit as a Christmas gift. Soon afterward I had my first contact with American musicians. Mr. Eugene List and his wife, Carol Glenn, gave an excellent concert in Budapest. He was the first person who played for me the wonderful preludes of Gershwin. After that, I played them all the time.

We were invited to a number of parties. One of them I remember particularly well. It was given by the American cultural attaché, Mr. Riegel. As usual, we did not eat that day. We knew that we would get a real meal in the evening, so we saved our ration cards. By the time we arrived I had a slight headache from hunger. The evening started with the maid bringing in a large tray filled with glasses, with some sort of yellow liquid in them. I drank down mine quickly and thirstily. Zoltán Kodály, the famous composer, was standing next to me. He asked: "What do you think you are drinking, Agi?" I said: "I don't know. It looks like orange juice. It tastes good." He replied, "It is not orange juice. It is an American cocktail" It took four or five cups of coffee to sober me up.

❧

In March 1946, Imre began to work at the university on a biological research project with Professor Szent-Györgyi. This was the first time in years that he received kindness, understanding, and support from a Hungarian scientist. He kept working on this problem until we went to Sweden some three months later. I shall never be able to thank Professor Szent-Györgyi enough for restoring to Imre his self-confidence. He began to feel again that there are some good people in the world after all.

During these months we never stopped telling Harry Le Bovit how fervently we desired to go to America. One day in May, Harry called Imre to his office and told him that he had good news for him. He had written a letter to Captain Dietrich, the US Navy Representative on the Allied Control Commission for Hungary, telling him that he was acquainted with a capable Hungarian scientist, Imre Patai, who has many interesting ideas. Captain Dietrich transmitted the letter to Commander Stephen Brunauer, who at that time was attached to his office on temporary duty. Commander Brunauer became interested, called up Harry, and asked him to request Imre to come to see him. He suggested that he bring along a biographical sketch of himself and some of his more important publications.

A few days later Imre walked into Commander Brunauer's office and had a long talk with him. He came back as though he was walking in a trance. He told me, "The commander said that he might be able to get me to America. It would be wonderful if such a thing could happen, but of course it is only a dream." I asked Imre what kind of a man this Stephen Brunauer was. He paused for a moment and reflected: "You know, when I looked at him and spoke with him . . . if there had been an ounce of hope and confidence left in me, I would say that I felt it for this man. If there is anything in this life but disillusion, I would believe him. He almost inspired confidence in me."

ೞ

Eventually, we had all our papers for the emigration to Sweden, with one exception. We just could not get the Russian exit permit. It was extremely difficult to get their permission to leave the country. There were thousands and thousands of applications on file—we were not the only ones who wanted to leave the country—but the Russians were in no hurry. Then we had a lucky break. I was asked to give a concert for the United Nations Relief and Rehabilitation Administration (UNRRA) representatives in Hungary. It was held in a private home. The place was very crowded; there was a mixed American, British, Russian, and Hungarian audience. When I finished the concert a Russian officer came to me, thanked me for my playing, and started a conversation. He spoke German pretty well. He told me that he had been an engineer before the war, and his wife was a concert pianist. Some of the selections I played were the favorite concert pieces of his wife, and they brought back memories of his home. He asked me whether he could be of help in some way to me. I answered that perhaps he could help me: "For many months we have been trying to get the Russian permit to leave the country—and did not succeed." He smiled and admitted that he could help me—but he did not want to—because if I left he would not hear me play again. But anyhow, he gave me his address and told me to come to his office.

For a whole week every day I stood in front of the building where his office was but was not admitted by the guards. Then one day it occurred to me that once I had been saved by the magic word "*artistka*," so I decided to try it again. I went to the guard and said, "*artistka*." He became at once very nice and asked, "Harmonica?" I said, "*Da*," and he let me enter. The officer received me very cordially and said: "Well, well, for a whole week I have been expecting you. I began to believe that you do not consider it very important to leave the country." I explained to him what had happened. In a few minutes I had in my hands the exit permits for Imre and me.

We had now all the papers to leave. Imre immediately got in touch with Commander Brunauer and went to see him in his office. He wanted to find out whether it would prejudice his possibilities of getting to the United States if he went to Sweden now. Imre told him that if his chances were good of getting to America, and he would lose them by going to Sweden, then he would rather stay in Hungary. Commander Brunauer told Imre: "By all means, go to Sweden. It will make no difference at all as far as your trip to America is concerned." He assured Imre that he would do what he could after his return to the United States to bring him out.

Imre's lawsuit was still not decided at that time, but the prospects were very bad. This made it easier for him to leave Hungary. He asked himself the question: "What would I do if I win back my factory and laboratory? Would I leave Hungary then, or would I stay? It is difficult to start a new life in a different country without anything at the age of fifty. On the other hand, can I afford to remain in this spiritual vacuum, among narrow, gray, empty, and selfish people?" I am quite certain that we would have left the country even if Imre had won his lawsuit.

❦

A few days later our Swedish friends sent us a car to take us to Czechoslovakia. Through a letter of introduction by Mr. Magnus, we had become acquainted with the president of the Hungarian branch of SKF, and he was the one who extended us this courtesy. The night before we left Hungary, our American friends gave us a farewell party. The house where the party was held was in Buda on a mountainside, overlooking the Danube. Budapest below looked lovely and serene. Our friends told us: "Do not look at the city too long. You will be very homesick." Imre replied: "Never." But despite everything we had been through, we had a little pain in our hearts.

14

Friends in the north

The next morning we drove to Bratislava. There we had dinner at the home of a childhood friend of mine—he was my first love. In the SKF office in Bratislava we found sleeping car tickets to Prague, deposited there by our patron, Mr. Magnus. In Prague we found airplane tickets to Sweden, again deposited by Mr. Magnus.

In Göteborg Mr. Magnus was waiting for us. We had breakfast in the Grand Hotel, the like of which we had not seen for many years. It started with shrimp cocktails and ended with coffee and whipped cream. We told him our story briefly, and he said: "You two look just about as bad as I thought you would. I have rented for you a room at a summer resort for two months. My only request is that you do nothing but eat and sleep. At the end of the two months we will discuss your future." Imre asked: "What are we going to do later on?" Mr. Magnus replied: "Please, do not worry about it now. Just concentrate on regaining your strength." And he added: "We here in Sweden feel that we cannot do enough for the people who suffered as you have suffered. We had a relatively easy time here."

He took us in his luxurious car to Hindos, a beautiful resort on a big lake near Göteborg. He paid our bill for two months, gave us money, and said: "Now I am going to my summer place in Lapland. I always spend my summers with the Eskimos."

The next morning Imre wrote in his diary: "The dream continues. We awakened in a clean room that has windows, and we again ate a real breakfast." But he was not the kind of man who could stay completely idle for two months. He read books on physics, studied some more English, and wrote dozens of letters to our American and English friends. Somehow he felt intuitively that Sweden would not be our final destination.

Everybody in the little hotel was unbelievably good to us. It was hard to believe that we were not dreaming and that people could be really so kind. One incident illustrates especially well what I mean. A few days after our arrival in Hindos I was run over by a bicycle. A couple of hours after the accident the cook of the hotel came to our room with a big package containing bandages and candy. There were enough bandages there for four weeks. She said: "I went to Göteborg to get these for you." We asked her how much we owed her, and she replied: "Nothing. We have to help those who suffered from the Nazis."

The two months passed quickly, and we moved to Göteborg. Professor Rudbeck invited Imre to collaborate on a research project with him at the Technical University. He had just returned from America, where he had been invited by the Rockefeller Institute. Imre worked and studied day and night, and kept up his correspondence with the friends in America and Britain. Occasionally he wondered whether Stephen Brunauer still remembered him. But he did not write to him. After all, Commander Brunauer was a stranger—Imre had met him only twice—and he did not want to bother him.

I gave many concerts in Sweden. We were walking on air. One of the greatest events in our lives was when we sent our first packages of food to our family and friends in Hungary. We felt like human beings again; we were able to help others.

The months passed. In February 1947, Imre received an invitation from Ericsson, the biggest radio manufacturing concern in Sweden, to organize a research laboratory for them and be the head of it. When he came back from Stockholm, he asked me whether I would not mind to move to Stockholm. I said: "Of course not. You will have a grand opportunity there to have your own laboratory." We discussed the matter further, and Imre decided that he would go back to Stockholm the next day to sign the contract.

That evening we had dinner separately. I had dinner at our hotel because I was expecting a visitor on business; Imre went to his favorite restaurant. The evening mail brought a letter from America. On the envelope was the name of the sender, Stephen Brunauer. I tore the letter open in great excitement—this was the first and last time in our married life that I opened a letter of my husband's. It was an invitation for Imre to come to America to the George Washington University in Washington, DC.

I left my visitor and my dinner and rushed to Imre in the restaurant. When he read the letter he looked at me and said, "I wonder who is playing a practical joke on us." But it was true—we felt it was really true. There are some fine and trustworthy people in this world.

We went to Mr. Magnus with Stephen Brunauer's letter. We asked him what to do. We did not want to be ungrateful—to leave Sweden just at the time when we really could have given something to the country—but Mr. Magnus was as broad-minded a man as he was kind-hearted. He advised us to go to America. He said that such an invitation comes only once in a lifetime. And he told us, "If you are not happy in America, Sweden will always welcome you back."

The next day I gave a Chopin recital. The American consul and his wife were in the audience. During the intermission, Mr. Magnus, who knew them very well, brought them backstage, introduced us to each other, and told Mr. Corcoran that Imre and I would visit him the following day. Mr. Corcoran smiled and joked: "I am not going to give you a visa. If you go to America, I cannot attend your concerts."

Of course, he gave us visas immediately. It is impossible to describe the feeling of joy and pride we had when the American visas were in our hands. The dream was still continuing.

Our last problem in Europe was to get passages to America. Every passage on the Scandinavian Lines was sold out until April. Imre said, "I have waited fifty years to go to America, but I am not willing to wait five more weeks." Once more, Mr. Magnus helped us out. He obtained passages for us on a ship that left from Norway early in March.

Our trip was not as simple as we expected. For the first time in fifty years the fjords were frozen over, so we had to go to Bergen—to the open sea—by train. I had influenza with a fever of 103 degrees, but we would have gone if both of us had had pneumonia. On the train between Oslo and Bergen a lady was sitting opposite us. She was most elegantly dressed, with beautiful luggage, and I sat there in rapt admiration. Later we began to talk with each other. I found out that she was a cook in a little restaurant somewhere in Ohio. Imre said to me in Hungarian, "If a cook in America looks like this, then we need not fear about making a living either."

Around midnight the train stopped in a little town between Oslo and Bergen. The passengers of the SS *Stavangerfjord*—including us—all went to see the house where *Peer Gynt* was written. In Bergen we had our medical examination. Then we boarded the ship. The last thing we heard in Europe, as the ship sailed out of the harbor, was the Norwegian national anthem. But our faces were already turned toward a strange new country.

15

At last, safe in America

It was a stormy crossing. Imre and I had one of the very few disagreements of our married life. He loved the sea and even loved the storms; I found the voyage very trying and disagreeable. I spent most of the time in my berth. The swaying and dipping of the ship made me very unhappy. One evening, Imre insisted that I go with him to see a movie. He said that it was just the thing I needed to take my mind off my seasickness. He was wrong. The movie started with a shipwreck, so I rushed back to my room and spent the rest of the trip in bed.

We arrived in New York on March 18, 1947. The arrival in the harbor was one of the most thrilling experiences of our lives. When the symbol of freedom of the new world, the Statue of Liberty, loomed before us in its indescribable magnificence, we stood on the deck, arm in arm, tears streaming from our eyes. We did not cry when we left Europe.

It was very cold and windy on the pier when the ship docked, and we had to wait for hours until we got through the customs inspection. We did not mind it; we felt warm inside. They told us that it was impossible to get a hotel room in New York, but that problem was quickly solved for us, too. A porter approached us, and seeing that we were obviously newcomers, he gave us the address of a hotel. He asked us where we had come from and what was our place of destination. We told him, he wished us good luck, and we shook hands. In parting, he said: "You will be happy here because everybody is happy here." This was our first welcome to America.

A taxi took us to the hotel. The driver charged us seven dollars. We strongly suspected that he overcharged us, but Imre said, "I am so happy that I would gladly give him seventy dollars if I could afford it." The hotel itself was quite an experience. We got a room on the eighteenth floor. It was the first time in our lives that we lived that high up. The gigantic buildings of Manhattan made a tremendous impression on us.

Imre immediately called up Washington, but we had no luck. Dr. Brunauer was on a business trip in California. Dr. Van Evera was away from George Washington University for the weekend. So we decided to spend the weekend in New York. The only old friend we succeeded in contacting was Dr. Lax, a physician with whom Imre had worked on kidney stones many years ago. We met a few more distant European acquaintances. It was interesting to note that all the Americans we met in our two days in New York were exceedingly kind to us, but the European acquaintances were rather cool and discouraging. They told us how difficult life was in America, how bad the climate was, and so on. But Imre answered, "We are willing to face any hardship in a country where there is freedom."

On Monday we went down to Washington. A nice room was waiting for us there in the Blackstone Hotel. Dr. Brunauer had left word with his secretary to help us out, and Miss Fink found this room for us. That was not an easy job in those days in Washington. Imre went to the university and came home very happy and full of enthusiasm. Dr. Van Evera was extraordinarily kind to him. The only thing Imre regretted about the university was that it had such a small music department.

We both were struck right at the start by the beauty of Washington. I was slightly disturbed by the fact that my ability to express myself was so limited, but Imre had no such qualms—he

was full of vigor and optimism. The first evenings Imre enter-
tained himself by looking up Hungarian names in the telephone
book and calling up some of them. The first person he called was
Dr. Frank Horvath. Although a stranger, he immediately invited
us to his home. It turned out that his wife was a former concert
pianist. He himself later became our family physician. The next
day Imre hit upon the name of Elizabeth Rona. This was really a
find! Elizabeth was one of our tried and true friends of many years.
We visited her immediately, the result of which was that for the
second time she played a decisive role in my life.

Let me tell about the first time. In 1939, Elizabeth was in
Sweden on a fellowship, doing research on radioactivity. I wrote to
her and asked her whether she could get me invited to Sweden to
give a concert there. And sure enough, she did arrange an invitation for me. That first concert in Sweden resulted in my becoming
acquainted with Mr. Magnus. I wonder how our lives would have
developed had I not met Mr. Magnus then. The second time was
on this night in Washington. I complained to Elizabeth that I
could not practice because I had no piano. She answered, "Right
across the street from your hotel is the YWCA building. You can
practice there for 25 cents an hour." This 25-cent advice led to
my entire musical career in America. You will see later how it
happened, step by step.

The next Sunday morning a gentleman in a Navy uniform
knocked on our door. This was the first time I met Commander
Stephen Brunauer. He had just returned from his two weeks of
duty in California. He welcomed us most cordially and invited
us at once to his home. It was a wonderful feeling to have this
new friend near us, in whom we had complete confidence, and
upon whose advice we could always rely. He gave his advice and
help and support to Imre unfailingly, patiently, and generously
until Imre's death—and he remained a very dear friend of mine
afterward, to this day.

As I said before, Imre and I both fell in love with Washington
at first sight. Imre said that he would be content to live all his

life in this beautiful city, but things did not go entirely smoothly for him at the start. He was anxious to throw himself into work immediately, but there was no laboratory available for him at the university. It took several weeks until he was able to start, and these weeks of waiting felt like years to him.

In addition, we had money difficulties. The Blackstone Hotel was too expensive for our scanty finances. But the biggest cause of our downfall was a remarkable American institution: the drug store. I do not think that any foreigner can resist the temptation of buying things—when there are so many things to buy—and at such low prices. We bought everything we saw, from nail files to back brushes, and the little money we had was slipping through our fingers rapidly.

In his spare time Imre loved sitting in Lafayette Park, watching the people. It touched him that the American people, in spite of their wealth and balanced life, did not lose their contact with nature and with each other. Imre would watch them sitting there in the park, eating their lunches, feeding the squirrels and doves, having cheerful and animated conversations with each other, and he had a feeling of warmth in his heart.

He was also fascinated by the Washington trolley cars. He spent many of the evenings in the first weeks riding the trolleys with a map in his hands. He invited me to accompany him, and I went once, but only once. I did not like the rocking of the streetcar any better than the swaying of the SS *Stavangerfjord*. My own personal hobby was the shoeshine parlor. I looked forward with joy to Saturdays, when we had our shoes shined, and occasionally I even slipped in an extra shoeshine on one of the weekdays.

Imre's greatest delight was the incomparable Patent Office of the United States. While he was waiting for his laboratory to be ready, he spent most of his time there. His second favorite was the Library of Congress. We visited all the museums and art galleries, especially enjoying the Phillips Collection. We had a sort of sentimental attachment to it because our dear friends, the Bonbrights, had talked frequently to us about it back in Budapest.

Soon after our arrival Imre bought a small radio for us, and he insisted that I should listen two hours every day to the speaking programs, to learn English. Later on he regretted this insistence. I became a soap opera addict and, I confess, can listen to them interminably to this very day.

During our first week in Washington, we went to the Department of Immigration and Naturalization to apply for our first papers. The papers came about six weeks later. We felt immensely proud, happy, and secure.

ᘓ

I said earlier that my musical career in America started at the YWCA. I went to practice there every day, and I practiced until my quarters ran out. The pianos were in the basement in separate booths, and a woman collected the toll, admitted us, and locked us in—just about the same way as restrooms are operated in Europe. The upright pianos in the booths had been rendered practically toneless in an effort to make them as noiseless as possible.

Soon the day came when we had no more quarters to spend. I went to the office of the YWCA and asked them if they could not give me some odd cleaning jobs, in exchange for which they would permit me to practice on a real piano. The girl in the office became interested in me and asked about my musical background. When she found out that I used to give concerts in Europe, she gave me the name of Miss Pearl Vaughn, a lady who was interested in music and also in the YWCA.

I visited Miss Vaughn and asked her to help me get some pupils. She asked me how much I would charge for a lesson. Not knowing the situation here, I answered, "Would five dollars be too much?" She replied that it certainly would be too much—I might possibly get one or two dollars for a lesson.

I saw that she had a beautiful piano in the room. It was such a long time since I had played on such a piano, so I gathered up my courage and asked her permission to play a little. She graciously consented, and I played for a while. She listened attentively, and then she excused herself, saying that she would like to make a phone call. A few minutes later she returned and said: "My dear, you must not give lessons under ten dollars. But in my opinion, you should not give any lessons at all. You should give concerts. Here is the name of a lady who has two grand pianos. You can practice at her home an hour or so every day."

I went to the home of this second lady, Mrs. Parker, a most charming elderly lady of eighty, who received me cordially in her beautiful house on Decatur Street. I played for her, and the same thing happened as in the home of Miss Vaughn. She excused herself to make a few telephone calls. When she returned, she said, "My child, next week you will give a concert in my house. I shall invite some of my friends."

I came to her home again the next day and practiced for an hour. When I wanted to quit, she said: "Why do you stop? Go on, keep practicing." And she added: "You may come here every morning and stay until the evening. You may practice all day, if you wish."

When the weekend came she invited Imre and me for dinner. Very soon this most remarkable woman became not only my patroness, but also one of our closest friends. We spent almost every Sunday with her. She and Imre played duets on the piano, and they became ping-pong partners, too. I am not sure that I have met a woman half her age who could match the agility of Mrs. Parker.

The following week the concert was held in Mrs. Parker's home. There was a distinguished audience there, including Mr. Phillips of the Phillips Gallery, Mrs. Agnes Meyer, wife of the owner of the *Washington Post*, Countess Széchenyi, and others. The result of this concert was that Mr. Phillips engaged me for a recital at the Phillips Gallery, and the *Washington Post* engaged me to play on radio station WINX every Sunday afternoon for half an hour. And that was not all. A lady came up to me after I finished playing and asked me whether I would be willing to give a concert in her home, too. She admitted that she could not pay much—all she could pay me was five hundred dollars for the evening. By that time I was in a generous mood, so I accepted her meager offering.

When I gave this concert, a very tall and distinguished-looking gentleman came to me and introduced himself. His name was Brown. We talked about music, and he asked me whether I had ever played in Boston. I said, "No," and he remarked, "Well, you should play there." I asked him whether he was working here in Washington, and he said: "Yes, I am in the Navy Department." Only later did I find out, when I saw his picture in *Time* magazine, that he was Assistant Secretary of the Navy John Nicholas Brown. I met the Browns several times thereafter. Mrs. Brown once expressed to me her love of a little Mozart selection, so as a Christmas gift I made a little 50-cent recording of it and gave it to them. My last encounter with the Browns was last summer, after the death of my husband. I had no money—as usual—but I had an idea. I wanted to rent a boat and go down the Mississippi with my little chamber orchestra, and I wanted to stop every night at a different place to give a concert. Since I had no money to rent a boat, I thought I would ask the Navy to lend me one. I called Mr. Brown on the phone and asked him if he could lend me a battleship, or some sort of a ship, for the summer. He said that he would be glad to give me a ship, but asked if I would have the money to run it. That stumped me. I forgot to consider that the running of a ship must cost some money. Anyhow, it was a good idea. And, as a matter of fact, somebody in Holland is using the same idea this year.

❧

In the meantime, Imre got a laboratory space at George Washington University. He presented a number of problems to Steve Brunauer—by this time we called him Steve—and he picked out one on which Imre started to work. The problem was to produce a silver mirror, not on top of a glass plate, as it is usually done, but inside the glass plate. The advantage of such a mirror is that it cannot be rubbed off the glass, nor can it be dissolved out by acid fumes, or even by an acid.

Imre was not completely happy that this problem had been chosen, but he never gave an inkling to Steve about it. He told me that the problem involved quite a bit of chemistry, and he had always preferred physics to chemistry. I told him that I was completely confident that he would have results in a few months. This made him a little bit angry, and he said: "Don't say such things. You expect more than I am able to do."

However, I was right. In two or three months, Imre, working with a young assistant the university gave him, produced beautiful results for the glass problem. In his spare time he worked on patenting some of the ideas on which he had worked in Hungary and Sweden during and after the war. In the year he spent at George Washington University, he submitted five applications to the Patent Office, on five entirely different subjects. Unfortunately, it takes a long time before patents are granted, and Imre did not live to see the granting of any of them. Only a few weeks ago did the Patent Office grant two of his patents. One of these is for a new type of cathode-ray tube with oxide-coated cathode (U.S. Patent 2,505,909). The other is for a new kind of electron emitter (U.S. Patent 2,506,466). How happy he would have been if he could have seen these patents! The other three applications—one of them on his process of making silver mirrors inside the glass—are still pending.

⌒

Eventually, our housing problem was solved, too. We found a little house in Georgetown that we loved dearly. When we first moved into the house, we had nothing in it except two beds and a table. Our first visitor was Mr. Bishop, a leading lawyer in Washington. He later became a very close friend of ours, and he is now the administrator of Imre's estate. We had no chairs, so we sat on the floor. The kindly humor and tolerance with which he reacted to our "irregular" situation gave us the first indication that Americans consider the inner human values of much greater importance than the property that one owns.

I mentioned that I gave weekly concerts on the radio. The selections were announced and commented upon by Mr. Donald Engle. When I heard his comments on the pieces of music I played, I began to realize how utterly false is the proud boast of Europeans that "culture is only in Europe."

Pretty soon I got a teaching position in Washington. I heard that there was a vacancy in the Music Department of American University, so I applied for it. Mr. McLean listened to my playing and engaged me. I had a large class, and I had to give many lectures. It was pretty difficult for me as my English was not very good, but people were most understanding and excused me for my failings.

I am going to tell you one little incident about my English. In one of my lectures, I related a Greek legend about a tree in Heaven that grew no flowers but human hearts instead, the hearts of people who were good on earth. Once a musician came to Heaven. He was a good man, despite being a musician, and he was chosen to give his heart to the tree. At that point I meant to say: "He opened his shirt, took out his heart, and hung it on the tree." But my English failed, and I said: "He opened his shorts . . ." My touching story ended in a thunderous laughter. The story was lost, but I did not lose my job. In fact, my relations with my students became more friendly and informal after that incident.

At the end of the school year, I gave a concert at American University. The Brunauers, the Le Bovits, and the Van Everas were there, and many other friends. They all seemed to enjoy the pieces I played. At the end of the concert I gave a little speech, expressing my gratitude to America—and especially to Harry Le Bovit and Stephen Brunauer. We were all deeply moved. I shall never forget that night.

❧

Our first period in America, the Washington period, lasted less than a year. Imre could not get a well-equipped laboratory at George Washington University. His laboratory was in the Chemistry Department, and it had some chemical equipment in it, but it did not have the physics equipment he needed. Since the university did not have the funds to get the instruments, Imre—with the approval and support of Dr. Brunauer and Dr. Van Evera—began to look for another place. He negotiated with the Bureau of Standards for a while, but this fell through because he was not yet an American citizen. He negotiated with the University of Maryland, but that also fell through for some reason.

Then Imre met Dr. Lucian of Temple University in Philadelphia. Dr. Lucian invited him to join the staff of the Research Institute of the university, and he promised that Imre would get an excellently equipped laboratory there. We both hated the idea of leaving Washington, not only because we loved the city, but also because we had acquired many dear, warm-hearted friends there. Still, there was no choice. Imre was eager to get on with his work, so he finally accepted Dr. Lucian's offer. Since we were not quite certain how things would work out, we decided that I would stay in Washington for a while, Imre would move to Philadelphia, and we would visit each other during weekends.

At the end of January 1948, Imre moved to Philadelphia.

16

A final resting place

In Philadelphia, Imre took a room in a hotel. He did not know a single soul there to start with, except Dr. Lucian. However, Dr. Lucian was very kind to him, and he invited both of us to his home several times.

Soon afterward I had to go back to Sweden for a week's concert tour. I had made this engagement while we were in Sweden, and I felt that the only decent thing I could do, in return for the hospitality we enjoyed in Sweden, was to fulfill it. The day after my arrival happened to be the first anniversary of a music society that several Swedish musicologists had founded together with me in 1947. I had to make a speech at the anniversary meeting, and I chose for my theme the subject of musical culture in America. I pointed out to my listeners that it is a great mistake on the part of Europeans to think that musical culture is higher in Europe than in America. I also told them about a music club in Washington where five or six times a year great artists play for children and children play for the artists. This appealed tremendously to my Swedish friends. We organized right on the spot a music club in Göteborg for children, after the American pattern, and a week later I gave the opening concert of this club before a huge audience of children.

I gave many concerts and found a warm reception everywhere. When I played in Gőteborg and Stockholm, the staffs of the American Embassy and consulate attended and sent beautiful floral arrangements to me. After the Stockholm concert the ambassador invited me to tea. They treated me as though I had been an American artist, and with great pride and gratitude I accepted this honor. My Swedish friends began to get a little peeved at me and said jokingly, "You are getting almost as bad as a German. Just as they boast about the way they do things in Germany, you boast now about the way you do things in America."

When my ship docked in New York, according to the protocol I should have gone ashore with the second group of passengers. The first group to land are the American citizens, the second are those who have their first papers, and the third are the visitors. Without my knowing, one of the passengers, an American foreign service officer, had talked to the immigration officials on the ship and told them how I raised the prestige of America and American artists in Sweden. As a result, I was allowed to go ashore with the American citizens—and I landed in America the second time with a warm glow in my heart, a catch in my throat, and a few tears in my eyes.

ॐ

After my return we decided that I should also move to Philadelphia. Our number one difficulty there was again the housing problem. Dr. Lucian spent day after day going around with us, trying to find a house, without any success. Finally, we located a little apartment in north Philadelphia, but it was very small, it had only a Pullman kitchen, the beds were uncomfortable, and the place was very far from Imre's working place. I was again without a piano, but the dean of the School of Music at the university permitted me to practice there as much as I desired

I went to see the president of the Philadelphia Academy of Music, and asked for a job there, but he said that there were no openings. He added consolingly, "In Washington it is easy to make a career, but in Philadelphia it is almost hopeless." I went to the owner of the Philadelphia Conservatory and asked him for a job—the answer was the same. As to my giving concerts, he said: "If you have a thousand dollars, you can get a concert arranged for you." However, I had no such money. So for two days every week I went down to Washington, where I kept up my lecturing at American University, continued giving piano lessons, and every other week I gave a lecture for amateurs in the house of Mrs. Parker

In the meantime, Imre was not faring so well at Temple University either. The Research Institute gave him a nice laboratory room, but there was practically no equipment in it, and money was forthcoming for new equipment at a snail's pace. It looked as though it might take years before he could build a well-equipped laboratory, and at the age of fifty-two, Imre felt that he could not afford to wait for years.

Then a lucky break came to him. He became acquainted with a brilliant young physicist, Dr. Martin Pomerantz, who was working at the Bartol Research Foundation of the Franklin Institute based at Swarthmore. They took an immediate liking to each other, and Dr. Pomerantz invited Imre to give a talk at the colloquium of the Bartol Research Foundation; there he met the director of the institution, Dr. Swann, who liked Imre's talk very much—and he liked his personality, too. Dr. Swann showed the laboratory to Imre, had a long conversation with him, and in the end he asked him whether he would not like to come to the laboratory and join the staff.

Imre was faced with a difficult problem. The laboratory in Swarthmore was the kind of place he had always dreamed of. It was excellently equipped and had an outstanding staff of scientists. The atmosphere was most inspiring. Whereas he felt—as I said before—that at Temple University it would take years before satisfactory scientific working conditions would be established. Still, he did not like to make a change so soon after going to Temple. He was not the kind of person who liked to go from place to place, and was especially worried about getting a bad reputation in America for impatience and restlessness.

We talked the matter over thoroughly and came to the conclusion that Imre should go to the place where he could produce and create the maximum of which he was capable. However, before he made his decision he wanted to talk the matter over with Stephen Brunauer. He went down to Washington. They had a long discussion on the subject, the result of which was that we moved once again, to Swarthmore. A month or so before the move, my own situation in Philadelphia took a sudden upward turn. The president of the Philadelphia Musical Academy, Mr. Szanto, called me to him and asked me whether I would be willing to take over the master class in piano. It was an emergency situation, because his teacher had had to leave suddenly. I accepted the offer happily. I asked Mr. Szanto whether I would be allowed to give a few lectures, and I also told him that I wanted to have a little chamber orchestra of my own and give at least one Bach recital a year. Mr. Szanto was very dubious about both, but to make a long story short, I am currently giving thirty-six lectures every year at the academy, I have my own chamber orchestra and have already given three Bach recitals this year.

After moving to Swarthmore, we felt for the first time that we had arrived in a safe harbor. We had never met in our lives so many kind, considerate, and fine people, who judged their fellow human beings by their inner worth, rather than by their material possessions. Everyone in the laboratory worked to help us find a nice home, so we quickly located one, but we could have it only for a few months. It was a lovely house with a beautiful garden. And I finally had a Steinway piano at home.

The first weeks we were invited out practically every day by the scientists on the staff of the laboratory. Our most frequent hosts were the Swanns, and Dr. and Mrs. Swann quickly became like our own family. Dr. Swann is an excellent cello player, and he and Imre played frequently together, or else I played with him. The Swann children also became close friends of ours.

Almost every evening we went to the Bartol Library. Imre's laboratory room was next to the library, and after dinner he usually returned there to work. The library had an excellent grand piano, so I went along with him and practiced there. It was like the first years of our marriage, when in the evenings Imre worked at home in his private laboratory, and I practiced on the piano in the next room.

Pretty soon after our arrival at Swarthmore, Dr. Swann advised us to get a car. Imre went after it in his own systematic way, and week after week he devoted an hour or two every evening to looking at used cars. He talked with the owners of the cars and learned from them not only the life story of the car, but frequently even the life story of the owner. Thus he obtained a better insight into the psychology of the American people, a problem that interested him intensely.

Finally, we bought a car, an Oldsmobile, for two hundred and fifty dollars. Its owner, a worker in a radio factory, had kept it in excellent condition. The fact that a factory worker could run a car seemed miraculous to our European minds, to say nothing of possessing such a high-grade car. The owner told Imre that his third child was born a blue baby, and that he must sell his car now to cover hospital expenses. Although the car was not quite what we wanted—it was too big—we decided to buy it to help the blue baby.

Our first ride in the car was to visit the family of this factory worker. He had a neat two-story house, a radio, a nice little library, and beautiful children. We took the children chocolate, but we saw that they were unhappy over not having the old car any longer, so we felt it better not to visit them again.

The car rode beautifully—until I smashed it. Just the day before I would have gotten my license, while driving under the tutelage of Imre, I found myself in the middle of a telephone pole. I was not hurt, but Imre received a pretty bad injury on his head.

About a month later Imre's library arrived from Europe. The fifteen boxes contained not only our books, but also some of

Imre's laboratory instruments, as well as my soundless keyboard, a few tablecloths, a little silver, and so forth. Characteristic of the kindness of the people of Swarthmore, on a very hot day the schoolboys and schoolgirls and our friends came and worked for hours to help us unpack the boxes and to carry the books in from the garden to the house. The boys were excited to find rifle bullets in some of the books—I mentioned that the Germans used these shelves of books as a barricade against the Russians. With the library back in our possession, we felt now that our home was complete.

As the months passed, we became acquainted with more and more of the Quakers of Swarthmore. We attended their Sunday meetings regularly, and we were so deeply impressed with their religion that we intended to join them officially.

Aside from going to the Friends' Meeting, the rest of the Sunday Imre spent working in the laboratory. That was the place where he felt the happiest. Before we came to Swarthmore, Imre's idea was to save as much of our earnings as possible, so that in ten years we should have enough money to retire from employment. He wanted to set up a little laboratory of his own somewhere in California and tinker around in it for the rest of his life. But after settling down in Swarthmore, he said that he no longer desired to have a private laboratory or to live in California; his only wish was to live and work in Swarthmore the rest of his life.

In addition to his work at the Bartol Laboratory, Imre became a consulting physicist of the Franklin Institute. One of our happy moments was when we received the two little cards from the institute—I was also given a card, which enabled me to visit the institute as the wife of a member. Another happy moment was when Imre filled out his application for membership in the American Physical Society. Unfortunately, the membership card did not arrive until the day after his death.

Our friendship with Dr. Swann and his family was perhaps the happiest friendship of our lives. We had so many interests in common—the main ones being, of course, love of science and music. Dr. Swann did everything to help Imre along. He even made trips with Imre to put him in contact with scientists at other institutions. Once he went down to Washington with Imre to discuss with the scientists of the Bureau of Standards a research project that Imre had suggested. Another time he came down with us to Washington to attend a concert of the National Symphony Orchestra at the Watergate, where I was the soloist.

Thus externally and internally our lives were completely happy now. We loved our work, our friends, and our home. Imre thought that he ought to write a book about America for the American people, because he felt that they do not appreciate fully their good fortune. He told me: "We must try to open the eyes of the people here to help them see how happy they are." And he felt that in the next ten years he would produce the maximum of which he was capable—and more than he had ever produced before.

ઝ

In November 1948, we had to move into another house because our landlady wanted her home back. The house into which we moved had coal heating, which eventually led to the tragedy of Imre's loss.

When we moved, all of our Swarthmore friends came again to help us. I wonder whether our American friends realized how deeply we were moved by this act of kindness. Nothing would be farther from the European mind than to help a friend in such dirty and exhausting work.

Imre kept on working harder than ever. He now had an assistant and a laboratory technician. He loved them, and they loved him. Every night after he came home from the laboratory, he read, studied, and worked until 1 or 2 o'clock. Perhaps he should have taken things a little easier, but it was impossible to convince him of that.

One day Dr. Swann called me and said that Imre would stay with him for lunch. He invited me over too and promised a surprise. And who was there in his house but Professor Clay, Imre's friend and boss from the University of Amsterdam. You met him at the beginning of my story, and you meet him now . . . near the end.

On December 23, I went to Philadelphia for my last teaching day and last lecture of the year. Arriving there, I had an accident on the railroad and almost lost my left leg. On this occasion we met again what Imre called "the healthy and balanced attitude of the American people toward life." When they carried me into the hospital, and the nurse saw my smashed foot, she did not say, "How terrible," "How unfortunate," or "How sorry I am for you," but smiled at me and said: "There will be a lot of money in this for you." That certainly raised my morale a good deal. Then Imre came and took me home to Swarthmore. After he returned to the laboratory, he called me up and said: "The friends here say that you will get at least five hundred dollars." An hour later he called again and said: "It is up to a thousand dollars now." By the evening the estimate went up to ten thousand dollars, and Dr. Swann told me that I should be able to buy a beautiful house with the money I would get.

This accident of mine led up to the final tragedy. On Christmas Eve the furnace of the house broke down, and our place was very cold. Imre tried to fix the furnace, our friends tried to fix it, but they could not. We were tied to the house, because I was unable to walk. Despite the cold we had a very nice Christmas—our friends from the laboratory and the college came to visit us, and the warm glow inside us compensated for the cold outside.

We called the coal company, and Imre had a sample of the coal examined in the laboratory. The coal was all right, but the house remained cold. On New Year's Eve, Imre awakened me and told me that he was having a heart attack. This was the first time in more than two and a half years—since we left Hungary—that Imre had a heart attack. I called the doctor, and he came immediately. A few minutes after his arrival Dr. Baker began to feel faint, and he had to leave the room to go outside for a breath of air. In a moment he rushed back and threw all the windows wide open. He told us that the whole house was filled with coal gas, and that Imre had coal gas poisoning. He went down to the cellar and found that a gas pipe was leaking: that was the reason for our inability to heat the house, and also for the poisoning. He said that it would take thirty hours before the poison left our systems.

For twenty-four hours we stayed in the house with wide open windows, and Imre began to feel better. On January 2, he went back to the laboratory. On the morning of January 5, he did not feel well and decided to stay at home. At noon he had a very bad heart attack. The doctor come again and found that we had—in spite of the fact that the leaking pipe had been fixed—a second coal gas poisoning.

Dr. Baker stayed with Imre for three hours. Although he was a stranger to us, Imre's own father could not have treated him more kindly. Imre calmly discussed the situation with him and told him: "Dr. Baker, please do not excite yourself too much over me. I know that I have coronary thrombosis, and that I shall not survive this attack." He then discussed with the doctor the kind of treatment that would be best for him. After three hours Dr. Baker had to go, and a second doctor came and stayed for two hours. Then a third doctor came, Dr. Sayen, who also stayed several hours.

Around 10 o'clock the other two doctors returned, and the three of them held a consultation. They asked me to come into another room and told me that the maximum time Imre could live was forty minutes. In consequence of the thrombosis both of his lungs were filled with fluid, and the end appeared to be near. But Imre had a very strong will to live—he wanted to finish the work he had started. He fought back, and he won a temporary victory. All night the doctor, the nurse, our landlady, and I sat at his bedside and the miracle happened right before our eyes: Imre's lungs cleared up and his pulse became practically normal. At 6 o'clock in the morning he told us: "Let us go to the hospital now." We ordered an ambulance, and the nurse and I took Imre to the hospital.

At the hospital they told me that there was no hope that Imre could survive. The coal gas poisoning was fatal. Nevertheless, they did everything humanly possible to save him. Professor Wood came five or six times every day to look after Imre, and Dr. Sayen came several times during each night. Dr. Swann came every day and sat with me for hours, just outside Imre's door. The other friends came too, and they tried to help and console me.

Most of the time Imre was delirious. He lay in an oxygen tent, and in his delirium he thought that he was again in a Gestapo prison. He shouted that it was not right to sentence an innocent person to death. He destroyed his oxygen tent and jumped out of bed many times a day. Perhaps he could have survived if these attacks had not come. But the Nazis killed him. The German and Hungarian Nazis killed him—after three years delay—in Philadelphia. In his lucid spells he made little jokes and asked about what was going on in the laboratory. On the tenth day of his illness the doctor permitted Dr. Swann to enter his room. Although Imre had been in delirium just a few moments before, he immediately became rational when he saw Dr. Swann. A few tears trickled down his cheek when he greeted him, and he said: "I don't think, Dr. Swann, that I shall ever come back to the laboratory." Dr. Swann, fighting back his own tears, answered: "Papa Swann expects you back. Nobody can do your job."

The next day Dr. Swann came again, and Imre said jokingly: "I thought a great deal about what you told me yesterday and decided that I will return to the laboratory. Of course I will return to your laboratory." Then he smiled at me and continued in the same vein: "You know, Dr. Swann, I have been married to this girl for sixteen years, and she still does not know any physics."

On January 16, Imre contracted pneumonia, and the damage to his heart was too great to survive this complication. For three days he lay in a deep coma. We brought a piano close to his room—we thought that I might be able to reach through to his consciousness through music—but it failed. Imre died on January 19 at 11:15 at night.

eɔ

Following Imre's wishes, I donated his body to the university hospital for postmortem examination. I took his very fine microscope and gave that to the hospital for research on heart ailments. Then I returned to Swarthmore. All of Imre's friends and coworkers there mourned for him, as though they had lost a very near and dear relative.

Imre's remains were cremated, according to his desires and mine. I went to Dr. Swann and told him that I should not like to bury Imre in a cemetery—he ought to be in the place where he was so happy. I asked his permission to let me come at night and bury his remains under the windows of his laboratory in the garden. I knew that that was what Imre wanted. But Dr. Swann told me that it would be better still to keep Imre's remains in the laboratory building, in an urn. They built a little niche in the building and put the urn there, and a lamp is burning beside it day and night.

The Quakers came to me and asked me whether I would like to have a memorial service for my husband. I accepted it gratefully. It was held the following Sunday, and the meetinghouse was jammed full—Imre had so many friends. The Quakers do not have any music in their services, but this time they had a piano there for me, and I said farewell to Imre through my music.

Several people spoke. This is what W. F. G. Swann, British-born, great scientist of America, said about Imre Patai, the Hungarian physicist, who wanted to become an American:

> It is characteristic of the highest type of being that he is one who can be sensitive to nature's beauties in all the forms in which she presents them to us. Dr. Patai was a man endowed with a rich sensitivity for the appreciation of all that was around. In science he loved to meditate upon the ways of nature as well as upon the facts of nature. In music and the arts he was not content with the role of passive enjoyment. His active mind sought always

the critical and constructive approach. While absorbed in the specialties of his field of research, his interests ramified continually into all that was around him. Even in his illness he became interested in the application of his science to the problems of the doctors who attended him.

He combined a forceful personality with a strong underlying sense of humanity and a warm feeling for all who were connected with him. So closely were his ideals integrated with those of his beloved wife that we feel that he has not completely departed from us, but that in her a goodly portion of his spirit yet remains with us.

After the service, a lady whom I had never met before invited me to her house. Many of my friends came there, from Swarthmore and from out of town. In the evening, Mrs. Parker took me down to Washington. The next day I continued my teaching at American University and the following week in Philadelphia.

ॐ

Many of our friends wrote letters of condolence to me. Perhaps these letters are of interest only to the receiver. Still, I should like to ask your indulgence to let me give you here two of them. They illustrate as well as anything I could produce the effect Imre had on his coworkers.

The first letter was written by Dr. Wallace Frank, a colleague of Imre's, whom I had hardly known at all. Here it is:

Dear Mrs. Patai,

Please accept my sympathy at this time.

It had been my pleasure to have been associated with Dr. Patai in connection with our development of a guidance device for the blind. Without the construction of a proper source of radiation, the device could not work. Your husband did start research in that direction and actually produced new sources. It remains to be seen whether or not these are satisfactory, but if they are not, new ones will be slight variations of the old.

You may, therefore, find some pleasure in knowing that one of the things on which Dr. Patai was working will owe its success in no small measure to his contributions, without which there was certainly little hope. Fortunately, the development was a humanitarian one, which makes it seem all the more important.

I regret that I did not know Dr. Patai better as a person, but as a colleague he made a most important contribution to a worthwhile endeavor. We shall miss him and the help he gave, very much. I thought that you might like to know this.

Sincerely,
Wallace Frank

The second was written by Imre's laboratory technician.

Dear Friend,

As you may have noticed from the name inside I was once Dr. Patai's laboratory technician and have been working along with him since.

Now, too late, I realize and I should say, will as time goes by, realize more the opportunity your husband gave me when he allowed me to work under him at Bartol.

My one hope is that someday I can be able to help science progress as I feel Dr. Patai gave his life for his work to do this.

If I can be of any assistance to you please feel free to ask my help.

Sincerely,
Philip

ೕ

I donated Imre's library to the Bartol Foundation. After Imre's death—to this very day—the people of the laboratory have surrounded me with their warm friendship. I have the feeling that in a similar situation I would not have had as many friends in the old country as I have here.

The Bartol Laboratory will print a posthumous paper on the work of Imre. Dr. Pomerantz is doing most of the work on it.

Before his death, Imre told me, "Agi, promise me that you shall always love this country as your own—with all its faults. The main strength of this country is that its people have the courage to admit their mistakes and the good will to correct them." Then he asked me, "What will you do after I am gone?" There was a sad little smile on his kind face as he reassured himself, "Anyhow, at least I brought you to America . . ."

When I was recently operated on and needed blood, all the physicists of Bartol rushed to the hospital to donate blood for me. Now that I have more American than Hungarian blood in me, I really feel that I belong to the great American family. Without this feeling of belonging there would not be much worth struggling for. I do not believe that I could have survived the loss of my husband in the old country.

Afterword

A life in thirteen boxes

There it was—battered and bruised, an early twentieth-century, maroon-brown doctor's bag, mangled at one end holding secrets of war, love, and endurance. This is what I found in a box labelled number fourteen in the Bryn Mawr College Library's Special Collections Archive, on a sunny spring day in 2018, seventy years after Agi's arrival on American soil and twenty-one years after her death in 1997. It really should have been labelled as box thirteen, because box three had gone missing, somehow, between the short distance from my Great-Aunt Agi's house in Radnor, Pennsylvania, just a few miles away from Bryn Mawr, way back in the 1980s. Perhaps in the end she could not bear parting with its contents, or maybe it just was not labelled correctly and somehow actually did go missing. But what a loss. Box number three contained all of her compositions.

Agi Jambor, born in 1909, became a well-known child prodigy, performing piano concerts all around Europe before World War II. She had studied under the grand masters, Zoltán Kodály and Edwin Fisher, and won prestigious prizes. In 1933, she married the well-established physicist, Imre Patai, thirteen years her senior. But the glitter vanished, as you will have read in her memoir, culminating in a tenacious struggle for survival during the siege of Budapest.

I got to know Agi in the early 1960s in Pennsylvania. She had put her past of hunger, terror, bombs, bullets, and snowstorms behind her, and I, a young teenager, could immerse myself in her zany world of artists and musicians, fuelled by irrepressible energy. She had been practically penniless when she first came to the United States, but I found her living comfortably in a large converted barn with a huge double-height living room that housed two grand pianos, a harpsichord, and a marimba (a sophisticated form of xylophone Agi tried to bring back into favour). With a steady job as a professor of piano and director of ensembles at the distinguished girls' college, Bryn Mawr, she had filled the house with musical instruments, books, and artefacts. It might have appeared chaotic, but it was coherent. It formed a rich, cultural whole. The house was full of cats, a dog, and young protégés from the music schools where she taught.

It was a wonderful ménage. She was delightful for a young girl like me, who in typical adolescent fashion could not talk to her mother about politics or anything else that mattered. And she was good for the many young women under her tutelage, navigating the way through what was an exciting post-1950s world of feminism and liberation. Agi didn't burn her bra, but she did set an example of how a woman could live an exciting and fulfilling professional life.

Agi had relaunched herself as a concert pianist, too. Much loved by Eugene Ormandy, she played with the Philadelphia Philharmonic Orchestra and others already in the late 1940s, and soloed at Carnegie Hall. She even played before President Truman. It was a triumph, but as she confessed to me long afterward, also something of an embarrassment. As she came to the end of her performance, she realised to her horror that her dress had its Woolworth's price tag showing. But who really cared what a penniless but hugely talented refugee from war-torn Europe was wearing? She was not one to feel mortified for long.

Agi always kept faith with her values. She spoke out about wrongs wherever she saw them. She was not frightened of standing up to McCarthyism in a period when America succumbed to the witch hunt of liberals accused of treason, subversion, and promoting communism in the early days of the Cold War. Her voice carried well beyond what one might have expected from her diminutive body. Box number fourteen also contained a bright green bag that she had used to deliver papers to the FBI supporting her Hungarian-born, but longtime American citizen, scientist, and naval officer friend, Stephen Brunauer, who had helped her leave Hungary, but had since fallen foul of the McCarthy cabal.

Agi was distraught over the war in Vietnam. Not content with wringing her hands, she set up a foundation for the starving children in Vietnam and gave concerts to raise money for the provision of food. With her friend, the Nobel Laureate Albert Szent-Györgyi, she composed a remonstration to God for all the evils that have befallen the people on this earth. It is a haunting piece, full of anger and unanswered questions. It is titled *Psalmus Humanus*, and you can hear it by going to www.agijambor.org and clicking on Agi Jambor's music from the menu.

As well as composing, teaching, and performing, Agi pushed at the boundaries of research in musicology, especially in the field of ethnomusicology. She was a great advocate of forgotten instruments, especially the marimba. She wanted to see these instruments preserved, and she curated a number of important exhibitions in museums.

After the premature death of her first husband, Imre, she moved among film stars and briefly married Hollywood actor Claude Rains in 1959. The name may no longer be familiar to you, but everybody remembers the debonair French police chief Louis in *Casablanca*. He was an actor of the old school, and he wooed Agi with his eloquence. When she understood English better, Agi told me, she realised that every sentence of his courting was a quotation from Shakespeare. The verbal charm did not last long, however; the marriage ended in divorce a year later. She did not marry again.

Agi regaled me with stories of better times before the war, like when she scolded Einstein, who, master mathematician as he was, proved incapable of counting when playing violin sonatas with her. It was during this period, when she was in her early twenties, living in Berlin, that she became acquainted with Albrecht Haushofer. Agi did not tell me about her relationship with this brilliant geographer, diplomat, and author, but I discovered it from reading letters in the archive. Haushofer, who years later was imprisoned for a failed attempt on Hitler's life, was released from prison on the day Berlin was liberated by the Russians, only to be gunned down by marauding SS officers a few hours later. Haushofer's brother found his body a few weeks later and in the breast pocket of his coat discovered a book of poems, written in a minute script, the *Moabit Sonnets*, still in print today both in the original German and an English translation.

The publishing of the *Moabit Sonnets* had a complicated history. The first and rather poor translation was carried out by the American Army. Given to the troops, it was intended to show them that not all Germans were despicable—an important consideration for the victorious occupiers. The second translation was made by M. D. Herter Norton, a confident of Agi's and cofounder with her husband of the W. W. Norton & Company publishing house.

While Haushofer was in jail in the 1940s, Agi was dodging not only Nazi occupants of Hungary, but then Russians and local Hungarian fascists—members of the Arrow Cross. As you know, she buried her only child during the war three days after its birth. In the end, the doctor's bag held all—yes, all—their worldly possessions. Their very few pieces of ragged clothing had long been discarded, but some treasures remained inside this small bag. On that sunny morning in Bryn Mawr, I gingerly handled the case that had once contained Imre's spectacles, a matchbox, and a few miniature scientific instruments.

As I rifled through the boxes I saw themes emerge—triumphs followed by crises, a box devoted to all her playbills and favourable press coverage (I never did find a negative one, though they must exist), letters to professional bodies, grant applications, and notes for her lectures. Most striking though were the letters to and from her family and close friends. Like an email trail, she kept carbon copies of the letters she wrote, filed alongside the replies.

On my first day at the Bryn Mawr archive I asked that all thirteen boxes be brought up from the storeroom at once. The archivist suggested that bringing up a few at a time would be more manageable, but I thirsted to soak up every bit of Agi's life I could find—preferably all at once. I had studied the sixty-four-page guide to the contents, prepared by a wonderful archivist at Bryn Mawr, and admired its order, but I felt impelled to crisscross the decades, to see if I could answer questions like "What was she like before the war? Could I fill in the gaps after the memoir ended? Was she really as happy as I remembered her to be?"

The first box contains her most valued correspondence, from prominent individuals to professional and personal correspondence, ranging from 1949 to 1988. The second box contains writings and evidence of other scholarly activities. This is where Agi's copy of the memoir is lodged: "Not for bedtime reading" she had written by hand and in pencil on the first page. There were other, shorter attempts at writing about the effects of war on artists, notes intended for relatives and others. I found lecture notes on music and ethnomusicology. A miscellaneous folder contains documents about her interest and involvement in Japanese tea ceremonies in the mid-1960s. Somehow a few documents dating back to 1921 relating to Agi's mother, Olga Reis, and her music school had survived. They had found their way into the second box, but there is no comment from Agi on them.

Before box three disappeared, its contents had been itemised, listing numerous compositions, many of them dedicated to friends. My heart stopped when I saw "A series of short pieces," eight to be exact, "dedicated to my niece Frances." I do not think I was ever told of these, though they were composed in 1964. There is a hint in the archive descriptions that they were somehow linked to the *Psalmus Humanus* she was working on with

Szent-Györgyi. The Vietnam War was escalating and would get worse before eventually ending in 1975. My own political activism began in 1964, with the first of many demonstrations against the war—with strong support from Agi.

The next two boxes are essentially scrapbooks, invitations, and press clippings mingled with concert programmes, notes on religion and philosophy, cartoons from *Punch* magazine, Christmas cards and postcards, airline tickets and dog photos, coauthored articles, and diaries.

Box six holds the original tape recording of Agi's debut at Carnegie Hall in 1949, which you can now listen to on her website. More material showing the breadth of her interest in—just about everything—is in this box. In several letters Agi spoke of being interested in "synaesthesia," where one sense (for example, hearing) is simultaneously perceived by one or more other senses (such as sight or smell). All ideas that transcended traditional boundaries were of keen interest to Agi.

Boxes seven through nine contain Imre's diaries from 1936 to 1949. The twenty-eight volumes, held here and in the Holocaust Museum in Washington, DC, provide vivid reflections of Nazism and day-to-day accounts of living through the war. The boxes also include Imre's scientific papers in Hungarian, German, and English, as well as more personal papers.

Box numbers ten through fourteen contain the papers of her great friend Egon Orowan, the prominent MIT physicist, also of Hungarian origin, who died in 1989. He, too, was worried about the direction society was taking, and Agi spent a great deal of time during their nearly thirty-year close friendship helping with his magnum opus, *The Aging of Societies*, though it was never published, possibly deemed too left-wing for an American audience, or else because at that time this type of interdisciplinary approach to political, economic, and social ills was less appreciated than it is today. Several versions are to be found in these boxes, along with lengthy correspondence over the role of the intelligentsia, all of which reflect Agi's breadth of interests.

Toward the end of my two-week immersion in these carefully labelled boxes I came across references to a period in the 1970s when Agi was trying to find solace in psychotherapy. The name of the Swiss psychiatrist, Dr. Oscar Forel, known as the doctor who first diagnosed Zelda Fitzgerald's schizophrenia, comes up at regular intervals from the 1970s onward. Agi went on a number of his retreats during the summers at his mansion in St. Prex, overlooking the Lake of Geneva. Whether it was his particular brand of therapy or his appreciation of the arts as a truly Renaissance man remains unclear; however, what was patently evident was that Agi was suffering not only from mental torment, but also from long-term physical problems, conditions shared with many friends who had also survived the war. Leaving the corporeal issues aside, she was looking for answers to questions from within a dark place from which she could not escape. This was not the Agi I knew, who was bubbly and effusive, giving the rich contents of her mind and soul to all who came her way. This was the Agi still haunted by war and betrayed by postwar events that she abhorred. Nevertheless, her fighting spirit never left her, and she continued to protest where she saw wrong, and give guidance to others where she could.

I did not see much of Agi after the fall of the Berlin Wall in 1989. I had already been living in London, and in the 1990s my work took me east, not west, working for philanthropic foundations in Central and Eastern Europe. Although I am sure she would have qualms with how things are now, I hope she rejoiced then over the successive peaceful revolutions in those countries, including in her own Hungary, even though her health had deteriorated and the world was slipping away behind the walls of dementia. She was fortunate in having a friend in the psychiatrist and amateur musician Joseph Stephens. He arranged for her move back to Baltimore in 1987, where she had first lived in America forty years earlier—but this time with her two pianos and huge library. Stephens and his friends made music with Agi almost every day in her apartment. On the day she died, she told Joe that she had been the happiest woman in the world during the last eight years of her life.

Looking back, I try to imagine how Agi must have felt during the time I knew her best at Bryn Mawr, in a wealthy, well-tended, and safe American college after everything she had been through. I wondered what it must have been like to feel safe in her twilight years after the horrors she had experienced. Could anyone like me ever imagine a life where all my worldly goods fitted into a mangled doctor's bag, fleeing vileness from fellow countrymen as well as invading foreigners? Can there be life after such knowledge? Agi Jambor proved that on the face of it, yes, but not without caveats, and needing tremendous reserves of strength, astoundingly revealed in retrospect by the contents of those boxes.

Acknowledgments

Many people helped make the publication of this book possible. Adam Freudenheim of Pushkin Press suggested that I look for a home among the American university press world, and that's when I found Purdue University Press. Justin Race, the director, took a gamble with it, and I am very grateful. He and his team have been a delight to work with. Many months before that, Peter and Susan Woodford gave me encouragement when I still wasn't sure it would see the light of day. Peter helped greatly with the initial editing, which was minimalistic so as to keep Agi's voice. He's written a short appreciation of the memoir, which can be found on the Agi Jambor website at www.agijambor.org. I think Peter fell just a little in love with Agi, as have so many who have read the memoir. Marcus Ferrar helped with the book proposal and wrote a short piece introducing Agi, also on the website.

Director of Special Collections Eric Pumroy and his team at the Bryn Mawr College Library, were unstintingly generous with their time and attention. My squeals of delight each time I found something exciting in Agi's archives, piercing the silence that befitted the reading room, were indulged. David Barrett took great care in rekeying the copy from a photocopy of a fading photocopy of a text written originally on a manual typewriter. Gábor Tóth, the archivist at the Hungarian National Academy, kindly located for me some letters from Albert Szent-Györgyi to Agi, which she had donated to them after his death. Mika Provata-Carlone contectualised the significance of the memoir, making publication even more imperative.

Another delight was discovering at the Bryn Mawr archives that Agi has living relatives in Budapest. I contacted her nephew, Robert Schiller, in 2018, a sprightly man in his eighties, and was fortunate enough to meet his wife, Vera, before she passed away, as well as their two daughters, Mariann and Erzsebet. These are my relatives too, and they and their families have increased the size of my very small family significantly. Robert introduced me to Judit Katona, who coincidently was organising a memorial concert for Agi, held in 2019 at the Academy of Music where Agi had been a student. Judit's husband, Ferenc, was, quite independently, familiar with Imre Patai's papers and provided me with more context.

Finally, a tremendous thank you to my husband, David, who participated in the preparation of this book in every way, from taking the photos in the archive to creating the website to preparing the manuscript for submission. At each stage his contribution was both critical and crucial.

About the author

Agi Jambor was born in 1909 in Budapest, Hungary, the Jewish daughter of a wealthy businessman and a prominent piano teacher. A piano prodigy, she was playing Mozart before she could read and at the age of twelve made her debut with a symphony orchestra. She studied under Zoltán Kodály and was a pupil of Edwin Fischer at the Berlin University of the Arts. Arriving in Baltimore, Maryland, in 1947, she was widowed shortly thereafter. She became a professor of classical piano at Bryn Mawr College and was briefly married to the actor Claude Rains from 1959 to 1960. Agi's life in America was full of intellectual and musical abundance. She was active in opposing McCarthyism and fought against the Vietnam War, giving proceeds from concerts to her charity that bought food for Vietnamese children. She was much loved by students as a charming yet feisty role model. She died in 1997 in Baltimore.

About the editor

Frances Pinter, born of Hungarian parents in Venezuela, grew up in the United States. Only in her early teenage years did she meet her relative, Agi, who became her role model. Pinter made a career in academic publishing in London. In the 1990s she worked for the Open Society Institute, supporting independent publishing all across the post-communist region.